The Sweet Scented Rose

THE SWEET SCENTED ROSE

A TREASURY OF VERSE AND PROSE
SCENTED BY PENHALIGON'S

EDITED BY SHEILA PICKLES

LONDON MCMXCIV

FOR JILL

INTRODUCTION

Dear Reader,

I was brought up to love and tend roses; compiling this treasury of verse and prose has broadened my knowledge and appreciation of this exquisite flower.

The rose has long held its place as Queen of Flowers; it has been the inspiration of poets, the symbol of Christian virtues, the badge of kings and the flower of love. According to Greek mythology, the rose was created by Chloris, goddess of flowers, who asked Aphrodite to give it beauty, Dionysus to add a sweet scent and the three Graces to bestow charm, brightness and joy. Finally, Zephyr blew away the clouds so that Apollo, the sun god, could shine and make the rose bloom.

Aristotle and Virgil wrote of the virtues of the rose; Roman warriors crowned themselves with garlands of roses during their feasts and bathed in rose-water; and Queen Elizabeth I adopted the Tudor Rose as her emblem. It has remained the emblem of England ever since.

In the garden the rose has always been enjoyed by both cottager and prince. In 1581 there were only ten different species of rose. Since then, a multitude of new varieties has been introduced and the rose now has an enormous family, varying widely in character and form, as well as in colour and habit. Sadly, the rose has also been the victim of fashion. The Tea, Bourbon and Damask roses, with their unique scent so beloved by the Victorians, were scorned earlier this century in favour of Hybrid Tea roses providing a wide colour range from midsummer until autumn. These scentless long-stemmed specimens, bred for the benefit of flower arrangers, bear little resemblance to the old roses rambling over my garden walls. Happily, our fine rose breeders today are anxious to combine the choicest and sweetest specimens to satisfy all tastes.

I have included in this collection many classic pieces on the rose by celebrated gardening writers such as Gertrude Jekyll, Vita Sackville-West and Louise Beebe Wilder, and poems by Shakespeare, Shelley and Keats. Also included are less well-known writings which deserve to be read: extracts from Marion Cran's amusingly titled *The Garden of Ignorance* and *The Garden of Experience*, and pieces by S. Reynolds Hole, Dean of Rochester and a great rose grower, who wrote in 1901, 'He who would have beautiful roses in his garden must have beautiful roses in his heart. He must love them well and always.' Like so many things in this life, roses need sunshine, water, food and love, then they thrive.

There is no more peaceful place than a rose garden. In medieval times people believed in the efficacy of various scents as a cure for the ills of the body and the spirit. I have noticed how the scent of roses soothes a troubled mind; when I am tired I go into the garden and breathe in their scent to refresh myself. For those readers who live a city life and are unable to spend time in a rose garden, I have scented the endpapers of this book with Penhaligon's Elisabethan Rose perfume, in the hope that you will find time to sit in a quiet corner and read these pieces, absorbing the delicate rose scent and enjoying a feeling of peace and well-being.

Sheila Pickles, London 1994

LOVE'S ROSE

Hopes, that swell in youthful breasts,
　　Live not thro' the waste of time?
Love's rose a host of thorns invests;
　　Cold, ungenial is the clime,
　　Where its honours blow.
Youth says, The purple flowers are mine,
　　Which die the while they glow.

Dear the boon to Fancy given,
　　Retracted whilst it's granted:
Sweet the rose which lives in heaven,
　　Although on earth 'tis planted,
　　Where its honours blow,
While by earth's slaves the leaves are riven
　　Which die the while they glow.

Age cannot Love destroy,
　　But perfidy can blast the flower,
　　Even when in most unwary hour
　　It blooms in Fancy's bower.
Age cannot Love destroy,
But perfidy can rend the shrine
In which its vermeil splendours shine.

PERCY BYSSHE SHELLEY (1792–1822)

Armfuls of Roses

My own first recollections go back to the days when as a child I used to stay with my great-aunt Lancilla.

And whenever I smell those leaves I am instantly transported to her house, and in particular to the broad, sunny passage which led to the kitchen. The sun came pouring through the sloping glass roof, and there was a whole bank of the sweet-leaved geraniums, reaching well above my head. Pinching the leaves was always a joy, for the scents were so rich and so varied.

But my chief recollection of that garden is of roses. Cabbage roses and La France and Gloire de Dijon and Maiden's Blush, and if one gathered armfuls it seemed to make no difference. Those were the days when people filled their rooms with innumerable small vases of flowers, but my great-aunt, who went her own way entirely, loved to have big bowls of flowers everywhere, even in the passages of her house.

Eleanour Sinclair Rohde, from *The Scented Garden*, 1931

Roses in History

The Wars of the Roses no doubt stimulated the national regard for the Rose, but quite aside from their use as partisan emblems, many passages in contemporary writers go to show that in the Middle Ages Roses were the most popular flowers in England. In those days Rose-lovers had to content themselves with the six native species, for no aliens had yet reached our shores. The fifteenth century, however, witnessed the arrival of the Damask Rose and the Provence Rose, which soon became universal favourites, and by Shakespeare's time there were over twenty varieties that could be distinguished one from another.

Thus about this time we begin to find Roses not only in the garden, but in the storeroom, the still-room, and even strewn on the floor in lieu of carpets.

The amount of Roses consumed in these various forms must have been very great, but still there were enough left to strew the floors in the houses of the wealthy. In old-time domestic accounts which have been preserved we find the item "strewing Roses and herbs" constantly recurring. When there was a glut of Rose-leaves in the market they could be purchased for sevenpence or eightpence a bushel, but as a rule they realised considerably more than this.

For people who could not afford the luxury of Rose-strewn floors there was a perfume sold "to burn on coals to make the house as though full of Roses."

R. FORESTER FELTON, FROM *BRITISH FLORAL DECORATION*

THOU BLUSHING ROSE

THOU blushing rose, within whose virgin leaves
    The wanton wind to sport himself presumes,
Whilst from their rifled wardrobe he receives
    For his wings purple, for his breath perfumes;
Blown in the morning, thou shalt fade ere noon,
    What boots a life which in such haste forsakes thee?
Thou'rt wondrous frolic, being to die so soon,
    And passing proud a little colour makes thee.
If thee thy brittle beauty so deceives,
    Know then, the thing that swells thee is thy bane;
For that same beauty doth in bloody leaves
    The sentence of the early death contain.
Some clown's coarse lungs will poison thy sweet flower,
    If by the careless plough thou shalt be torn;
And many Herods lie in wait each hour
    To murder thee as soon as thou art born,
Nay, force thy bud to blow, their tyrant breath
    Anticipating life, to hasten death.

SIR RICHARD FANSHAWE (C. 1607)

The Parliament of Roses to Julia

I DREAMT the Roses one time went
  To meet and sit in Parliament:
The place for these, and for the rest
Of flowers, was thy spotlesse breast:
Over the which a State was drawne
Of Tiffanie, or Cob-web Lawne;
Then in that Parly, all those powers
Voted the Rose, the Queen of flowers.
But so, as that her self should be
The maide of Honour unto thee.

ROBERT HERRICK (1591–1674)

Arranging Roses

One of the best containers for roses is the tin-lined garden basket I have mentioned before. Old glass milk bowls, old Sheffield cake and bread baskets, simple rough pottery bowls, are all good, but I would never choose the silver-rimmed cut-glass rose bowls which still seem to have some measure of popularity.

For large parties I have used red roses most satisfactorily, abandoning the idea of tall decorations, and concentrating on masses of colour. These need to be placed at such levels that their beauty is not hidden. What you may lose of the spectacular value of tall flowers, you will gain in other ways. A mantelpiece, for instance, is a good point of vantage. I have made massed arrangements of red roses here in a ballroom. The roses, though really carefully arranged, looked as though they had been heaped there in careless profusion and almost at random, and, on a summer's night, this was particularly pleasant. For small supper tables, I have lighted each with a single large wax candle and surrounded the base with a mound of roses. It is not difficult to secure the candle in the centre of a shallow glass bowl so that the flowers may be in water. A similar arrangement is good on a long dark refectory table, and then, if you wish, you may put before each guest your menu written on a flake of mother-of-pearl laid in the heart of a single rose.

For a large dinner party, during the coronation festivities, the table was covered by a white satin table-cloth and on this red roses were massed in the form of the cross of Saint George, extending the full length and breadth of the table, so that it looked as though it were covered by this ensign. The flowers were laid on a bed of moss, from which the cloth was protected by a layer of waterproof paper. The flowers, of course, were not in water, but they lasted easily throughout the party and afterwards were flung into water to recover. The next day they were fresh again and were arranged in shallow bowls for the house.

CONSTANCE SPRY, FROM *FLOWERS IN HOUSE AND GARDEN*, 1938

The Fragrant Rose

FRAGRANCE is the rightful heritage of the Rose, and it is what we consciously or unconsciously expect of it. We cannot dissociate fragrance and the Rose. If you doubt this, watch the visitors at any Rose show bobbing forward automatically before each exhibit to inhale the fragrance and plainly registering by word or look pleasure or the reverse at the response they receive. Beautiful as is the Rose it is only half appreciated by the eye; the nose has a great part in our delight in it and ever has had. In times long gone when the Rose was a simple flower, not eclipsing the elegance of the Lily, nor the showiness of the Tulip, it was known as the Queen of Flowers, as it is to-day. Surely it was the lovely quality of its fragrance, with which no flower can compete, that gave it this prestige.

But this *old* Rose scent is not by any means the only fragrance that belongs to this versatile family. There are, as a matter of fact, many types and degrees of Rose sweetness, as well as a complete lack of it in some varieties, and in a scant few an actually disagreeable odour. It is said that experienced Rosarians are able to identify many kinds of Roses in the dark, or with their eyes shut, which goes to show there are many distinct types of fragrance among them. "Indeed so capricious is the nature of this perfume and so extraordinary the complexity of its forms, it is claimed that not only in the whole list of Roses are there no two that develop the same odour, but that in the same species, and even on the same plant, there are not to be found two flowers exactly identical as to odour, and yet further, that it is a fact well known among Rose growers that at different times in the day, or of its development, an individual flower will emit a different perfume."

Warmth and moisture are important factors in Rose fragrance, as with other flowers, though the presence or absence of either cannot be said to determine whether or not a specific variety is to be classed as especially fragrant. It will be noticed that on cool days, especially if the weather is dry, that the perfume of the Roses in the garden is perceptibly less strong than on warm ones, and it is well known that Roses blooming under glass, or when brought into a warm room, are far more fragrant than those flowering in the open air, and more readily give off this perfume to the air. A still, moist and mild atmosphere is the most favourable to fragrance in any flower.

LOUISE BEEBE WILDER (1878–1938) FROM *THE FRAGRANT PATH*

Modern and Old-Fashioned Fragrances

The fragrance of the rose is probably more mourned when it is missing than that of any other flower, but it apparently would be inaccurate to say that modern roses are less fragrant than old-fashioned roses. Bertram Park, an English rose authority, writes in his *Guide to Roses*:

> Nothing irritates me more than the question "Why have modern roses lost their fragrance?" . . . There are two or three hundred species of roses . . . from which our modern roses have descended; of these only a half a dozen or so are fragrant. In spite of this handicap, the hybridists have succeeded in bringing out fragrance in modern roses.

The truth seems to be that, not counting the species roses, there are quite a few old roses without scent or with very little scent, and we all know there are plenty of new ones. There is a difference, however, in the fragrance of the old and the new. Each type of ancient European rose had its distinctive and beloved scent – damask, gallica, musk, alba, centifolia, and so on – whereas the scent of modern roses has become mixed by an infusion of many strains. This may be one cause of the mutterings about today's hybrids. I suspect, though, that the chief basis for complaint about their loss of scent derives from the prevalence today of the floribundas, many of which are still far more floriferous than they are sweet-smelling. We grow them for other reasons than scent. Even so, each year the rose men develop a few new fragrant floribundas.

Katharine S. White (1892–1977) from *Onward and Upward in the Garden*

A Bowl of Roses

'S PRING' says your Alexandrian poet
'Means time of the remission of the rose'

Now here at this tattered old café,
By the sea-wall, where so many like us
Have felt the revengeful power of life,
Are roses trapped in blue tin bowls.
I think of you somewhere among them —
Other roses — outworn by our literature,
Made tenants of calf-love or else
The poet's portion, a black black rose
Coughed into the helpless lap of love,
Or fallen from a lapel — a night-club rose.

It would take more than this loving imagination
To claim them for you out of time,
To make them dense and fecund so that
Snow would never pocket them, nor would
They travel under glass to great sanatoria
And like a sibling of the sickness thrust
Flushed faces up beside a dead man's plate.

No, you should have picked one from a poem
Being written softly with a brush —
The deathless ideogram for love we writers hunt.
Now alas the writing and the roses, Melissa,
Are nearly over: who will next remember
Their spring remission in kept promises,

Or even the true ground of their invention
In some dry heart or earthen inkwell?

LAWRENCE DURRELL (1912–1990)

THE ROSE

O ROSE, thou flower of flowers, thou fragrant wonder,
   Who shall describe thee in thy ruddy prime;
   Thy perfect fulness in the summer time;
When the pale leaves blushingly part asunder
And show the warm red heart lies glowing under?
   Thou shouldst bloom surely in some sunny clime,
   Untouched by blights and chilly Winter's rime,
Where lightnings never flash, nor peals the thunder.
And yet in happier spheres they cannot need thee
   So much as we do with our weight of woe;
Perhaps they would not tend, perhaps not need thee,
   And thou wouldst lonely and neglected grow;
And He Who is All-Wise, He hath decreed thee
   To gladden earth and cheer all hearts below.

CHRISTINA ROSSETTI (1830–1894)

The Gardens of My Youth

THE gardens of my youth were fragrant gardens and it is their sweetness rather than their patterns or their furnishings that I now most clearly recall. My mother's rose garden in Maryland was famous in that countryside and in the nearby city, for many shared its bounty. In it grew the most fragrant roses, not only great bushes of Provence, Damask and Gallica roses, but a collection of the finest teas and Noisettes of the day. Maréchal Niel, Lamarque and Gloire de Dijon climbed high on trellises against the stone of the old house and looked in at the second-story windows. I remember that some sort of much coveted distinction was conferred upon the child finding the first long golden bud of Maréchal Niel. Once a week, on Friday, a great hamper of freshly cut roses was loaded into the back of the "yellow wagon" – its physical aspect in no way bore out its sprightly name – and with "old Tom" in the driver's seat we fared into the city and distributed to the sick, the sad and the disgruntled, great bunches of dewy fragrant roses. . . .

LOUISE BEEBE WILDER (1878–1938) FROM *THE FRAGRANT PATH*

My Luve Is Like A Red, Red Rose

My Luve is like a red, red rose,
   That's newly sprung in June:
My Luve is like the melodie,
   That's sweetly play'd in tune.

As fair art thou, my bonie lass,
   So deep in luve am I;
And I will luve thee still, my Dear,
   Till a' the seas gang dry.

Till a' the seas gang dry, my Dear,
   And the rocks melt wi' the sun;
And I will luve thee still, my Dear,
   While the sands o' life shall run.

And fare-thee-weel, my only Luve!
   And fare-thee-weel, a while!
And I will come again, my Luve,
   Tho' 'twere ten thousand mile!

ROBERT BURNS (1759–1796)

To A Friend Who Sent Me Some Roses

As late I rambled in the happy fields,
    What time the sky-lark shakes the tremulous dew
  From his lush clover covert; – when anew
Adventurous knights take up their dinted shields:
I saw the sweetest flower wild nature yields,
    A fresh-blown musk-rose; 'twas the first that threw
    Its sweets upon the summer: graceful it grew
As is the wand that queen Titania wields.
And, as I feasted on its fragrancy,
    I thought the garden-rose it far excell'd:
But when, O Wells! thy roses came to me
    My sense with their deliciousness was spell'd:
Soft voices had they, that with tender plea
    Whisper'd of peace, and truth, and friendliness unquell'd.

JOHN KEATS (1795–1821)

The Queen of Flowers

THE Rose Garden must be a garden of Roses only. We do not plant shrubs around our oaks, and no birds may warble when the nightingale sings. It is the palace of the queen, and though she rejoices in the society of her subjects elsewhere, she brooks no rival near her throne.

The walks should be entirely of grass, and, where it is closely mown and well rolled, it is always available as a dry and delightful promenade for those persons who do not prefer wet weather for the enjoyment of their love among the Roses, and would regard it as disrespectful to appear in goloshes before the queen of flowers.

These walks must be broad in proportion to the beds, as in the Great Garden. There is no frame so appropriate as the grass for the most beautiful of all pictures, the flowers.

S. REYNOLDS HOLE, FROM *OUR GARDENS*, 1899

One of the Loveliest Scenes

Enter, then, the Rose-garden when the first sunshine sparkles in the dew, and enjoy with thankful happiness one of the loveliest scenes of earth. What a diversity, and yet what a harmony, of colour! There are White Roses, Striped Roses, Blush Roses, Pink Roses, Rose Roses, Carmine Roses, Crimson Roses, Scarlet Roses, Vermilion Roses, Maroon Roses, Purple Roses, Roses almost Black, and Roses of a glowing Gold. What a diversity, and yet what a harmony, of outline! Dwarf Roses and climbing Roses, Roses closely carpeting the ground, Roses that droop in snowy foam like fountains, and Roses that stretch out their branches upwards as though they would kiss the sun; Roses 'in shape no bigger than an agate-stone on the fore-finger of an alderman,' and Roses five inches across; Roses in clusters, and Roses blooming singly; Roses in bud, in their glory, decline, and fall. And yet all these glowing tints not only combine, but educe and enhance each the other's beauty. All these variations of individual form and general outline blend with a mutual grace. And over all this perfect unity what a freshness, fragrance, purity, splendour!

S. Reynolds Hole, from A Book About Roses, 1869

QUEEN ROSE

The jessamine shows like a star;
    The lilies sway like sceptres slim;
Fair clematis from near and far
    Sets forth its wayward tangled whim;
    Curved meadowsweet blooms rich and dim; –
But yet a rose is fairer far.

The jessamine is odorous; so
    Maid lilies are, and clematis;
And where tall meadowsweet flowers grow
    A rare and subtle perfume is; –
    What can there be more choice than these? –
A rose when it doth bud and blow.

Let others choose sweet jessamine,
    Or weave their lily crown aright,
And let who love it pluck and twine
    Loose clematis; or draw delight
    From meadowsweet's clustry downy white; –
The rose, the perfect rose be mine.

CHRISTINA ROSSETTI (1830–1894)

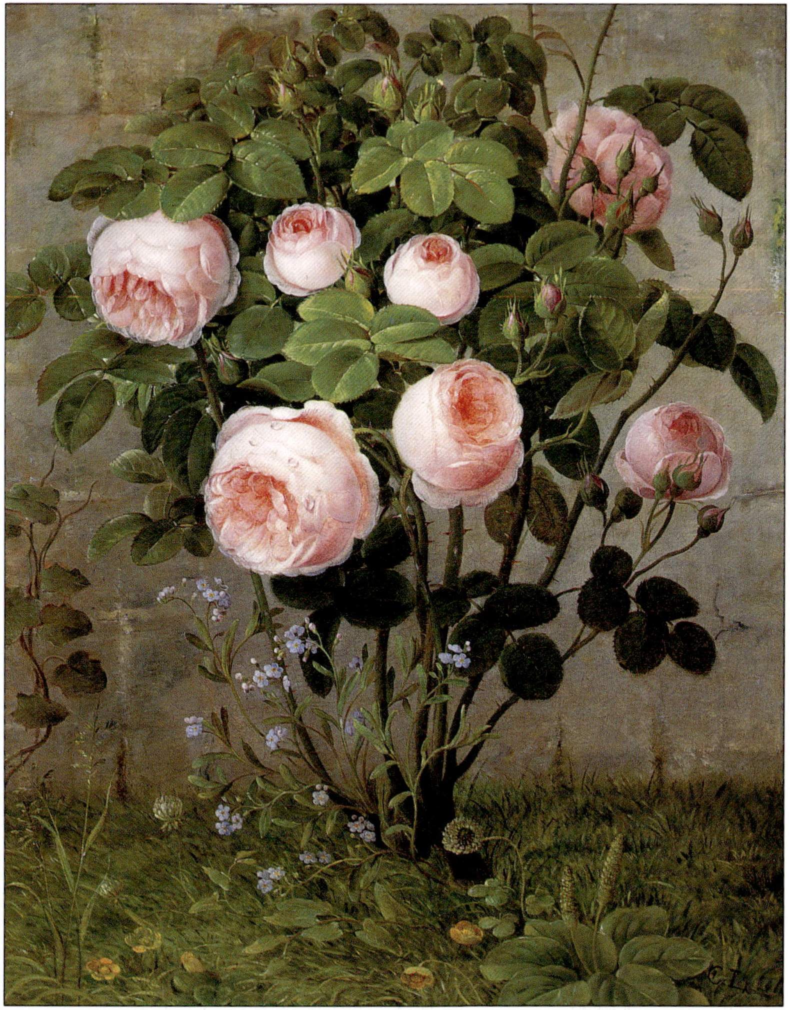

Formal Rose Gardens

Sometimes the Sunk Garden is used chiefly for one particular flower – for Roses, Irises, or for Tulips. Often, however, a special formal garden is created for the culture of the flower that the owner fancies most. Of these single flower gardens, the Rose Garden is undoubtedly the most popular, because of the long season of blooming that the Rose gives, as well as its ease of culture. A Rose Garden is definitely among the labour-saving features of a garden, and needs less attention than mixed flower borders, or beds of annuals, for example.

There are other reasons for growing Roses in one special part of the garden. The Queen of Flowers is haughty, and does not mix well with other plants, except the very dwarf kinds, such as pansies and violas. Roses like plenty of air, ample sunshine, and good soil. And they display best against a background of green grass. This makes it advisable for the Rose Garden to take the form of a number of small beds, set in grass paths, or grass-edged paths, an arrangement which has a double advantage in that it eases the work of pruning, cutting, and hoeing.

So, from various causes has grown the idea of the Rose Garden, which is now generally made in formal design, with small beds, each containing a group of one variety. Relief to the flat appearance of such a garden can be found in the erection of pergolas and pillars, and the use of Standard Roses.

Richard Sudell, from *Landscape Gardening*, 1933

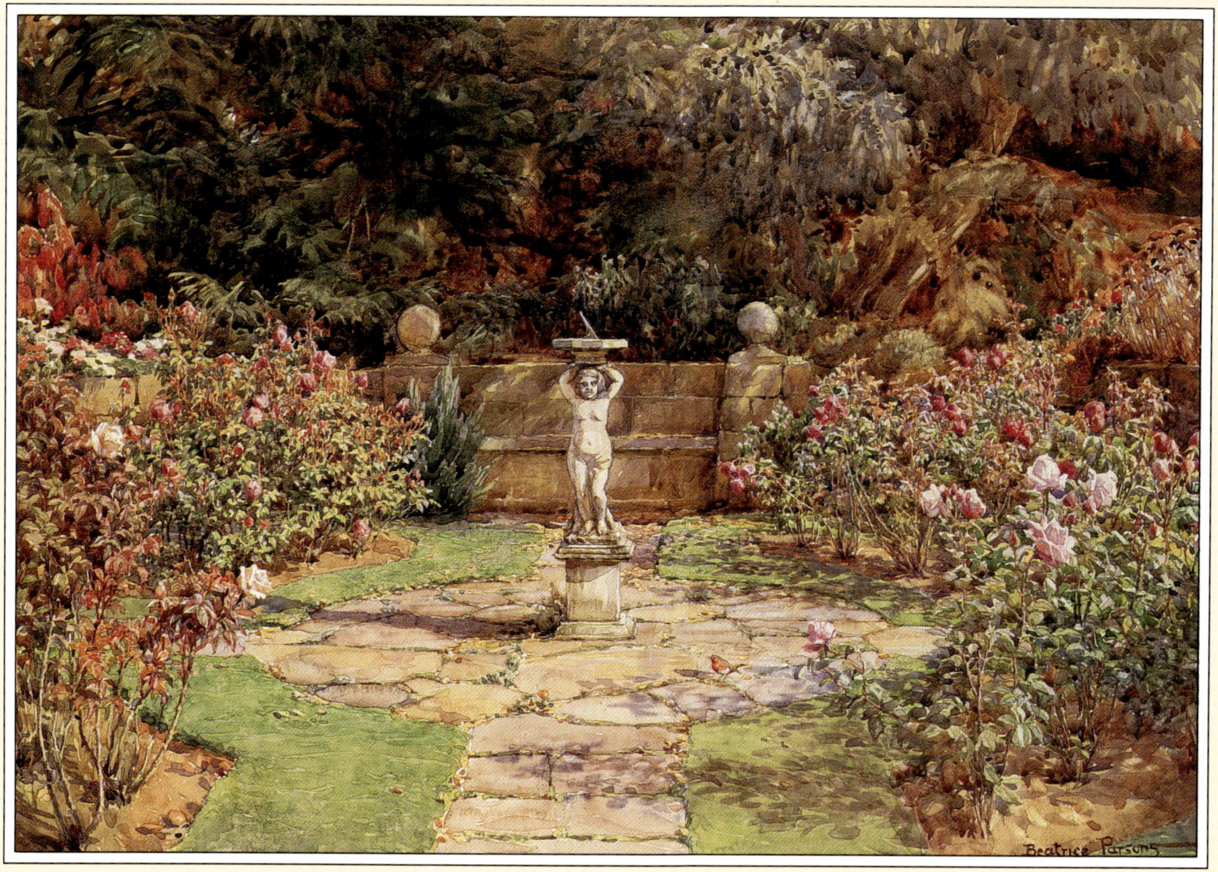
Beatrice Parsons

Splendid Isolation

An English garden without Roses would be an incomplete and soulless thing. I do not say that every garden should include in its design a Rose garden. There are, however, many advantages in allotting some portion of the grounds mainly to the culture of Roses, and it is almost inevitable that sooner or later some part of the garden becomes known as such. Not the least advantage of this giving over one portion of the garden to Roses is the fact that the results obtained thereby are, generally speaking, far more satisfactory than by attempting to grow them mixed up with other things. The Rose is one of those plants that thrives best in a state of splendid isolation. It objects to being associated with anything else. It needs a sort of special treatment that is not applicable to many other garden flowers. This exclusiveness on the part of the queen of the garden would almost seem to extend to its commercial associations. There are many firms who specialize in this or that, but I do not recall a single instance where there are a number of firms devoting their entire attention to the culture of the plants of one particular genera as in the case with Roses.

It will, however, be universally conceded that the Rose is worth this exalted position in the garden. What else is there that gives us such variety of form and colour, such an extended period of blooming, such adaptable habits of growth that there can be found, sorts that will climb over a house and cover the roof with flower, or provide a neat and glowing edging to a border, and achieve almost everything the garden requires in between these two extremes? It is because they are sufficient in themselves for most garden purposes that they have appropriated a place in the English garden that is held by no other flower.

George Dillistone, from *The Planning and Planting of Little Gardens*, 1920

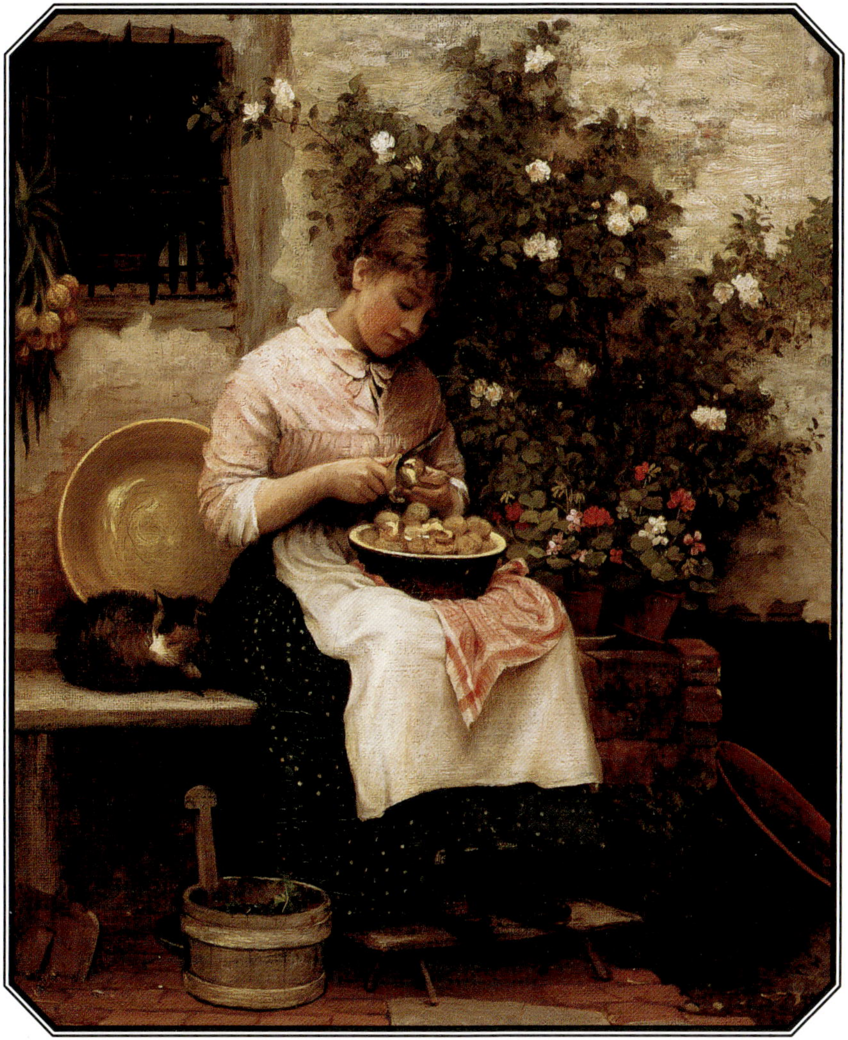

THE ROSE

A ROSE in the garden slipped her bud
    And smiled in the pride of her youthful blood
As she saw the gardener passing by –
"He's old, so old, he soon will die,"
    Said the Rose.

And when morning came with sunshine bright
She opened her warm red heart to the light,
And sighed as the gardener passed the bed –
"Why he's older still, he'll soon be dead."

But evening closed with a cold night air
And the petals fell from that rose so fair,
And when morning dawned came the gardener old
And raked them softly under the mould.

And I wove the thing to a random rhyme –
For the Rose is Beauty, the gardener Time.

R. FORESTER FELTON

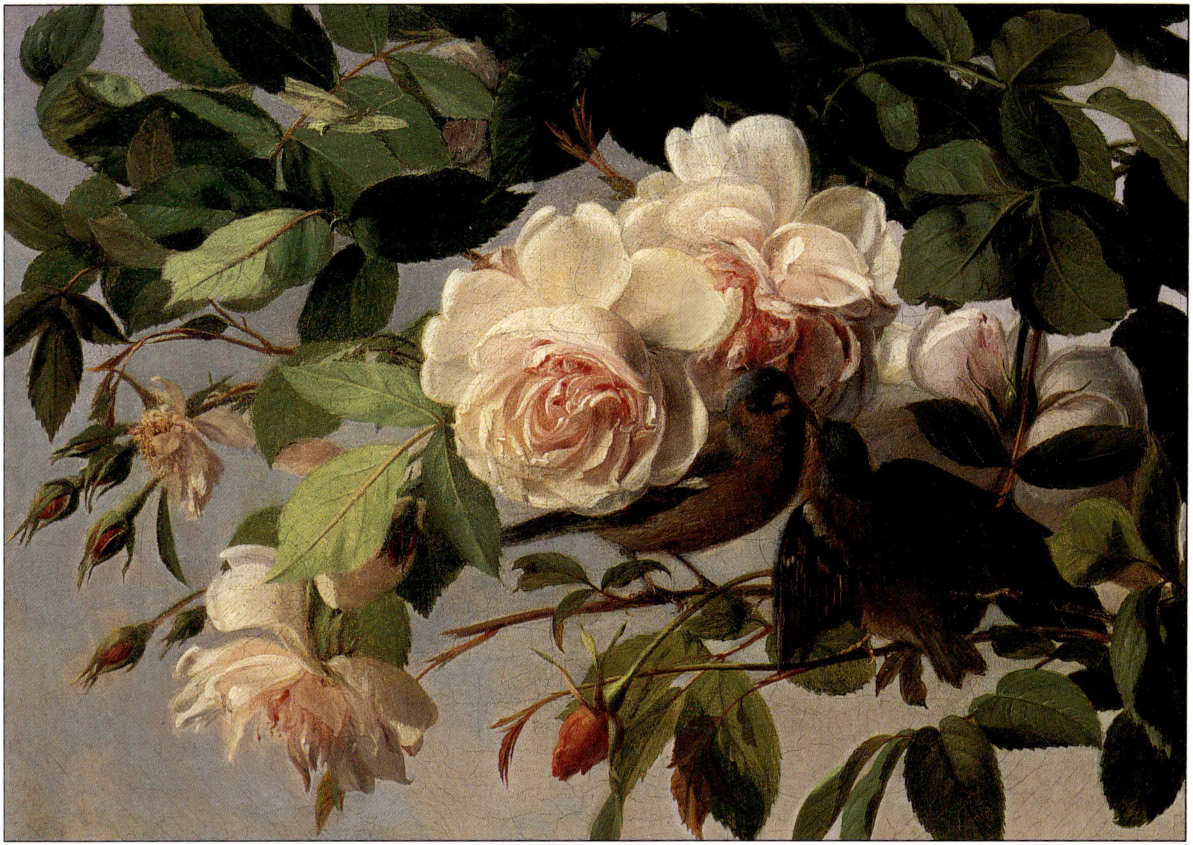

The Crimson Rambler

In our ideal garden, the entrance to the Rosary is either from the lawn between the shrubberies, or from the terrace walk down the steps, but such arrangements must vary in accordance with the formation and surroundings of the beds. There can be no more beautiful approach than the pergola, which was covered, when I saw it, with *"the Crimson Rambler,"* with Tea roses on either side. In some convenient corner of the Rose Garden there should be a bower, boarded and roofed and floored, with seats and table, containing drawers for catalogues and tools, and a cupboard for the crockery of five o'clock tea.

S. Reynolds Hole, from *Our Gardens*, 1899

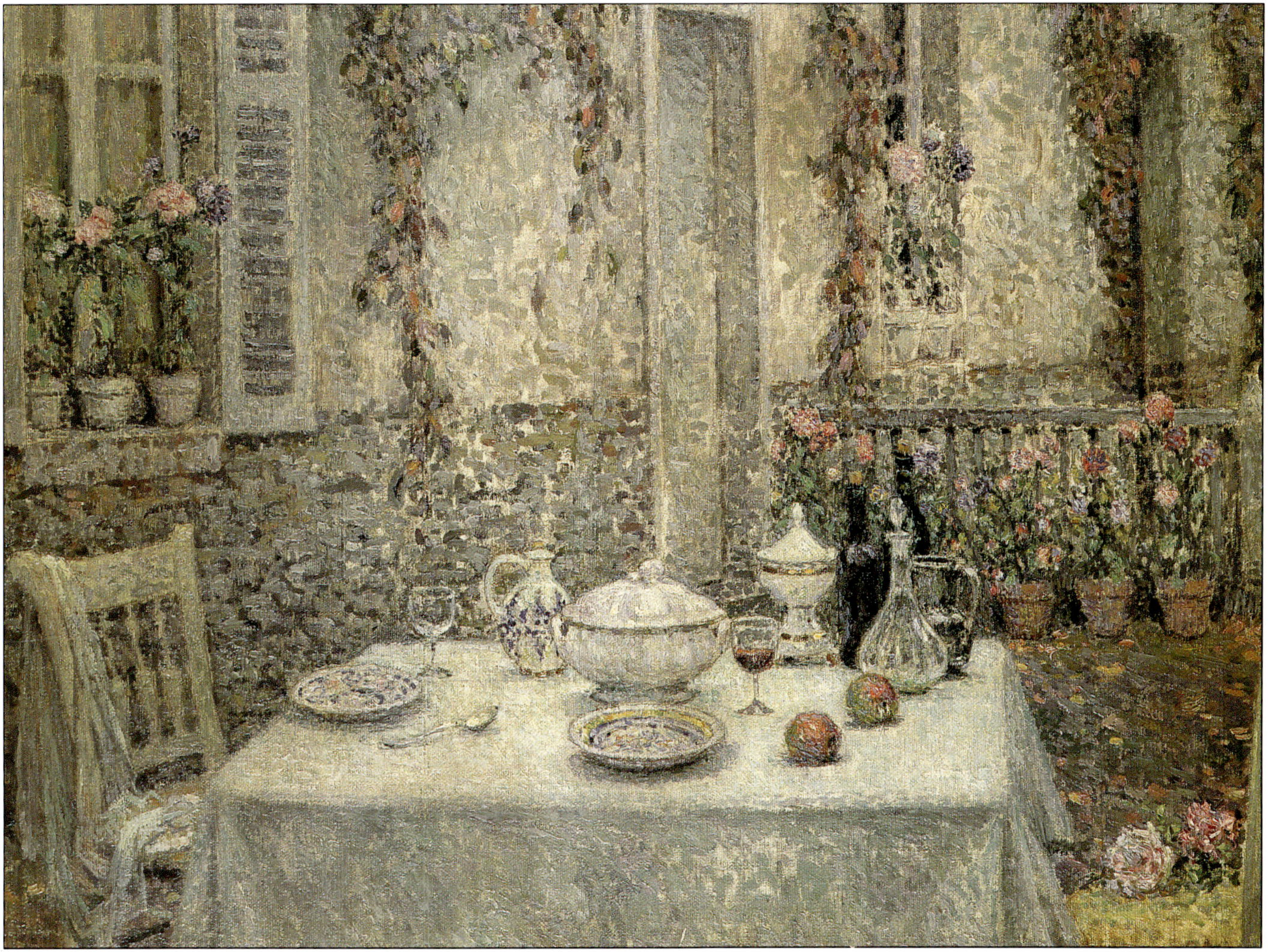

Song of the Rose

If Zeus chose us a King of the flowers in his mirth,
   He would call to the rose and would royally crown it,
For the rose, ho, the rose! is the grace of the earth,
   Is the light of the plants that are growing upon it.
For the rose, ho, the rose! is the eye of the flowers,
   Is the blush of the meadows that feel themselves fair, –
Is the lightning of beauty, that strikes through the bowers
   On pale lovers who sit in the glow unaware.
Ho, the rose breathes of love! ho, the rose lifts the cup
   To the red lips of Cypris invoked for a guest!
Ho, the rose, having curled its sweet leaves for the world,
   Takes delight in the motion its petals keep up,
As they laugh to the Wind as it laughs from the west.

Elizabeth Barrett Browning (1806–1861)

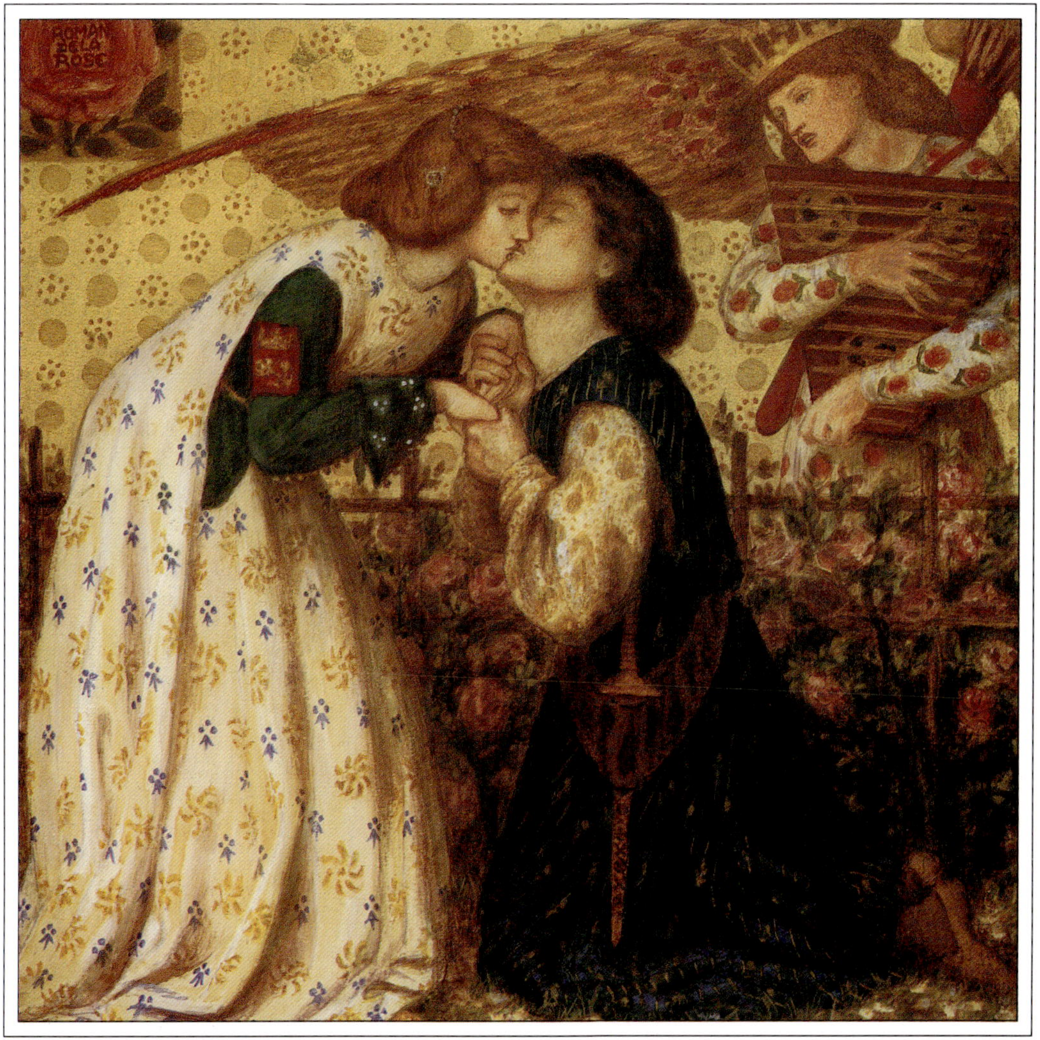
ROMAN DE LA ROSE

Perfect Ignorance

No one could really have started rose-growing in more perfect ignorance than I. Looking at the sandy desert which surrounded the cottage four years ago, I bethought me that roses climbing and scrambling everywhere would be a pleasant change, so I walked off across country, through hopfields, to a nursery I had heard of, in order to collect some rose trees. It was with surprise I learned that July was not the best month in which to transplant things from the open, and that if I really must have roses at once, to bloom at once, they must be roses out of pots. Four was all I thought I could carry at that rate; and it will be long before I forget the toilsome return over the interminable hopfields carrying four hefty flower-pots. Nor will I readily forget the planting of them: a little hole dug in the dry hot sand, the plant turned out of its pot, put in, and then well watered in the blazing sun with a good can of ice cold water off the main. Every error the willing fool can commit I made in planting my victims. A highly unsuccessful rose harvest, coupled with some glimpses of other people's roseries, led me to buy Dean Hole's book on roses, and there I learned the fatal glibness of the early endeavour. Soon I knew enough to envy with all my heart and soul those lucky folk who have a rich loamy soil over clay, where roses cannot *help* growing if the drainage is sound. They never grow well where their roots are waterlogged. The drainage in my garden is excellent but everything else is wrong.

Mrs Marion Cran, from *The Garden of Ignorance*, 1924

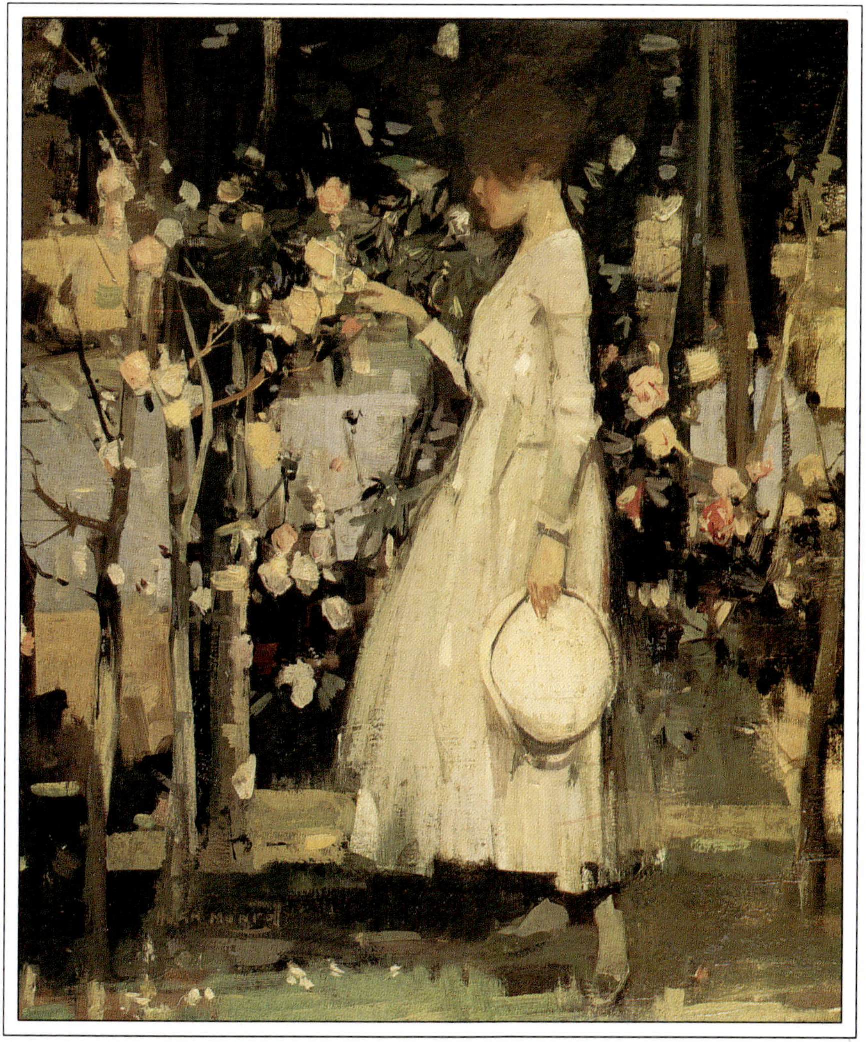

On Pruning

March 26, 1950

We now approach the time of year when the thoughts of Man turn towards the pruning of his roses. Knives and secateurs are now at their sharpest. Brandishing these objects of destruction, battalions of professional and amateur gardeners advance, prepared to do their worst, as they have immemorially been taught. The word of command has gone out: 'Cut almost to the ground; cut down to the second or third bud; cut till nothing is left except a couple of inches sticking up. Be pitiless, be ruthless; prune for fine blooms, exhibition blooms, even if you don't intend to exhibit. Never mind about the appearance of your garden, or the natural alacrity of your roses. Snub them as hard as you can, even as Victorian parents snubbed their children.'

It rejoices me to see that different ideas are creeping in. The rose, even the hybrid Teas and the hybrid Perpetuals, is no longer to be regarded as a stunted dwarf, but as a wildly blossoming shrub. Let her grow up, even to three or four feet in height, and throw her head about as I believe that she was meant to. This truth first dawned upon me during the war, when as a Land Army representative I had occasion to visit many small gardens in pursuit of owners who had been called away. Their gardens were turning into a sad disorder of weeds, but the roses reared themselves up, superb and proud, just because they had not been interfered with for two, three, four, five years. Then in the well-kept garden of a friend I saw similar rose bushes which, she assured me, had scarcely been touched since she planted them thirty years ago. She had merely snipped the tips; had taken out the dead wood and the weak growth; and for the rest had left them to their will. The result was lavish and surprising.

My liking for gardens to be lavish is an inherent part of my garden philosophy. I like generosity wherever I find it, whether in gardens or elsewhere. I hate to see things scrimp and scrubby. Even the smallest garden can be prodigal within its own limitations, and I would now suggest that you should try the experiment of NOT slaughtering your roses down to almost ground level, at least for this year; and see what happens.

VITA SACKVILLE-WEST (1892–1962) FROM *IN YOUR GARDEN*

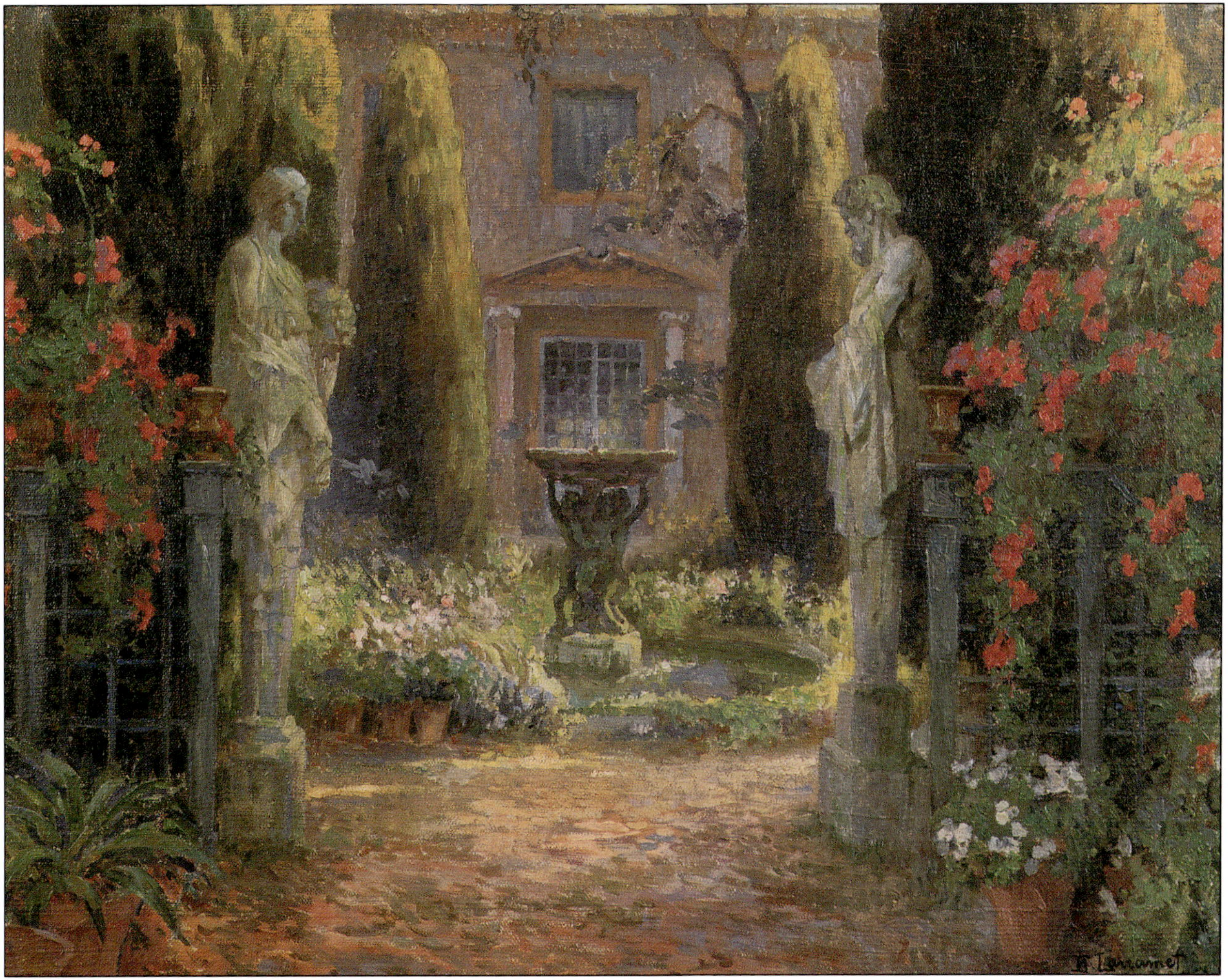

Among the Rambling Roses

In my Garden of Ignorance I used to make a very great mistake at first among the rambling roses. I was mean about pruning. I got close-fisted and hated to part with old wood. I could not trust the amazing vigour of the roots to fling up fresh leaders year after year, and I played around in a lady-like manner with a pruning knife, behaving as though I had met a group of tea roses in need of attention. And so, of course, the bloom grew spare and sulky, and the abundance of succulent green crowned with great heads of lusty bloom which I saw in other people's gardens never came my way at all. I complained bitterly, and was warned by wise-acres about my mistakes, but somehow autumn after autumn I dallied and minced among the old wood, unable to trust.

One day a friend put a powerful pair of sécateurs in my hand for a birthday gift, remarking that all that rubbish in the roses wanted something stronger than my little knife. The size and strength of the instrument went to my head, I believe, for I passed to the nearest Dorothy Perkins and shore every strand to the ground, shutting my eyes as I did it, and gave up the roses for lost. The harsh treatment gave the rambler the exact fillip it needed; next spring it was a maze of strong green, and in July bore excellent shoots. So I learned my lesson. And now every December, when the last beloved bud has bowed to frost, I go round and cut with ruthless vigour. In a more reasonable frame of mind, truly, for I do not now shave the whole structure of the ramblers to the ground, but cut out every bit of wood that has bloomed, leaving only the lusty young virgin shoots to bloom next season, and of those I leave the strongest and the best. The ramblers are immensely grateful for manure water through May and June, and amply repay the trouble such fare involves.

Mrs Marion Cran, from *The Garden of Experience*, 1922

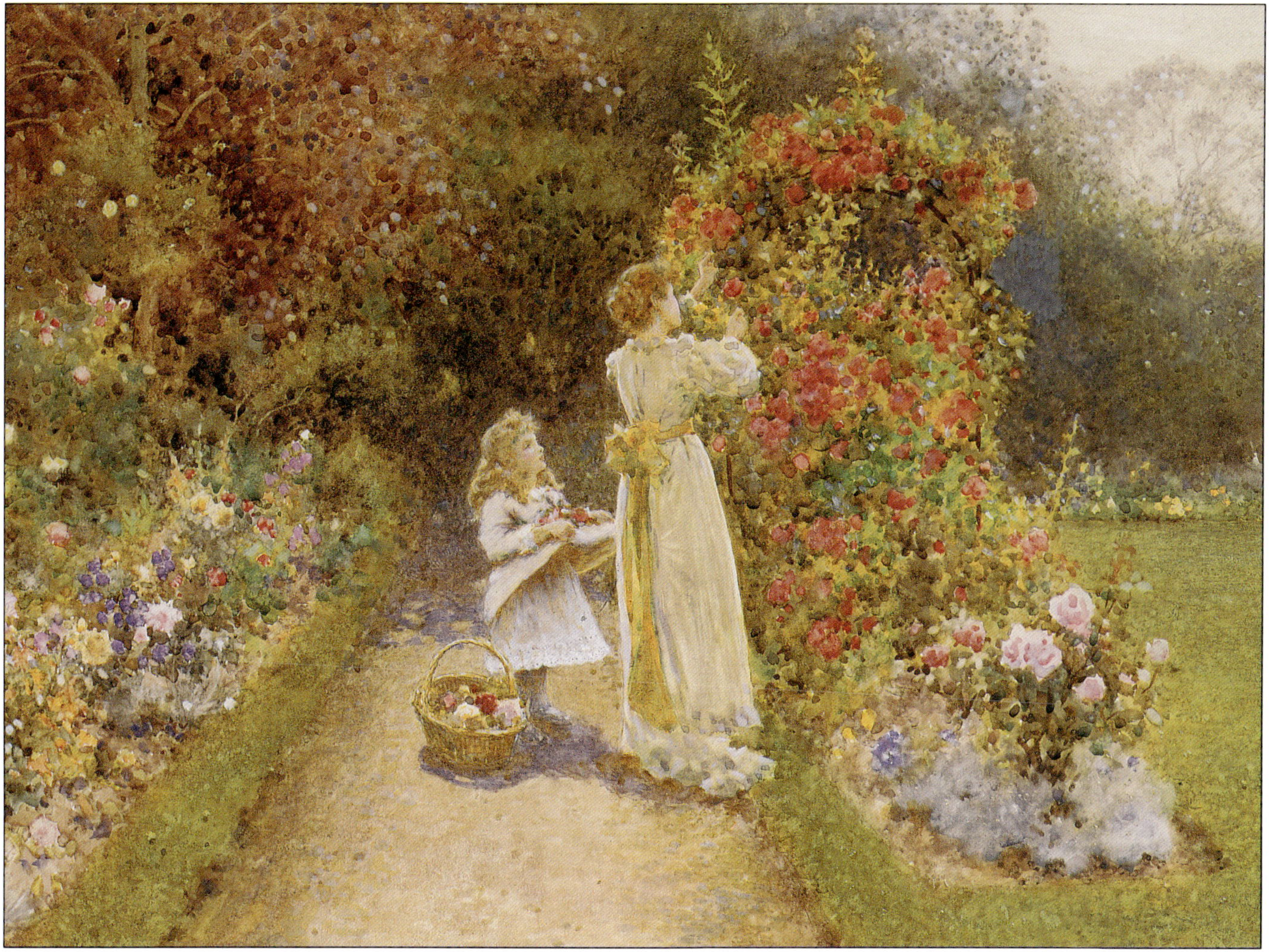

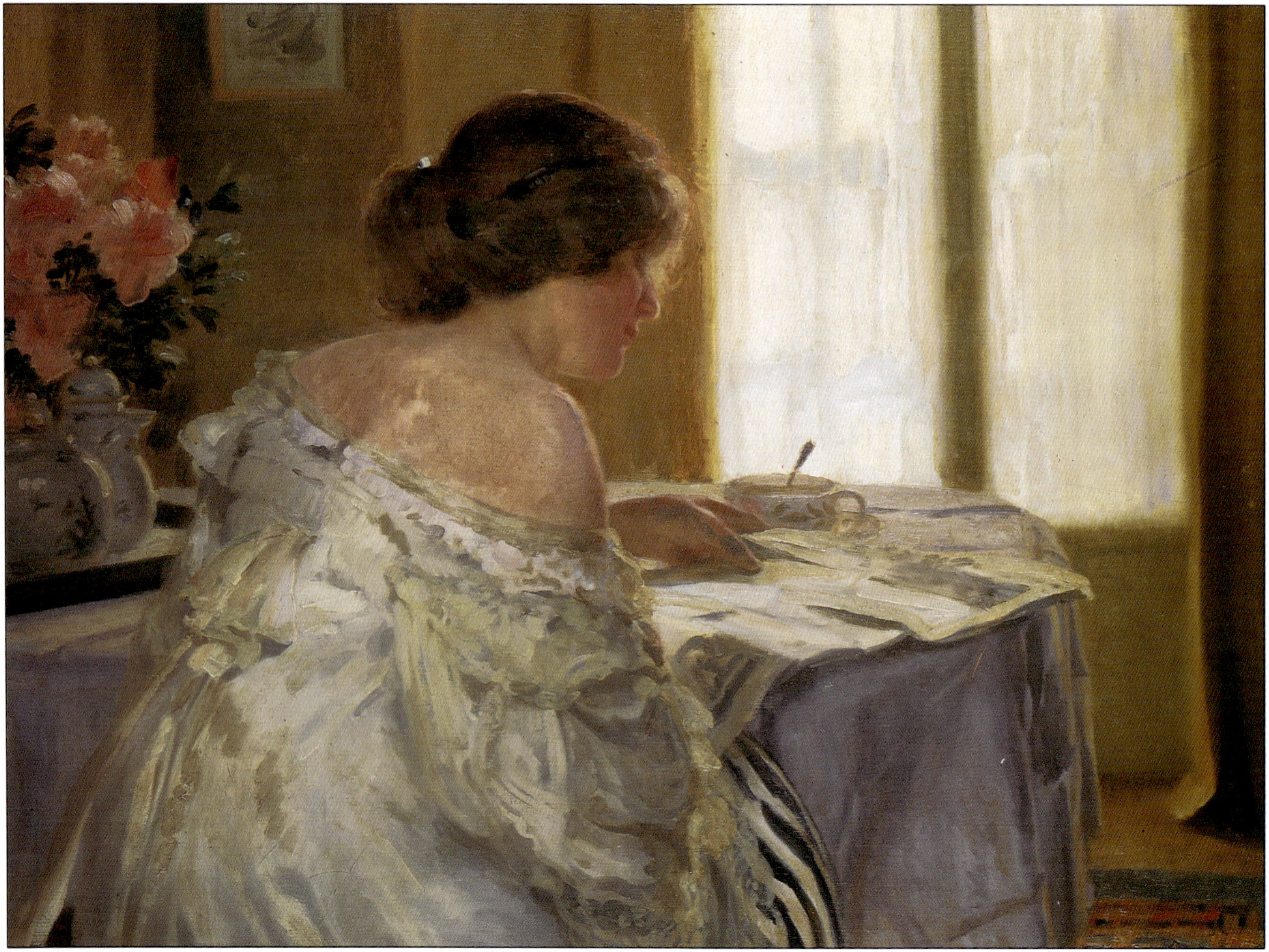

A Guide to Planting

SELECTING roses is by no means a simple matter. As a rule the more inexperienced the amateur, the more rash he is in his selection.

Therefore to all beginners I would say, state your requirements to an expert, and leave the selection to him, or else visit the rose grounds of some leading nurseryman, and see them growing.

Order your plants in the height of the rose season. Visit a nursery, an amateur's rose garden, or a rose exhibition, make notes of what you would like to get; compile your list with regard to the capacity of your garden, and despatch the order at once. While the rose fever is at its maximum is the best time to order roses; do not delay until the autumn, or you may have cooled down – at least this is my experience. By sending the order early you will probably obtain better plants, and also be more likely to get what you want; you can always add to your first order later on. It is the usual practice of the trade to execute orders in the order in which they are received – first come first served.

On the arrival of the plants the bundle should be carefully unpacked, and the roses 'laid in by the heels'. To do this dig a trench in some more or less protected spot, say in the kitchen garden, and lay in the plants side by side, the removed earth from the trench forming a back on which they may slightly lean. If there are more roses than will fill the first trench, or indeed in any case, dig another trench parallel to the first, and turn the earth as it is taken out into the first trench, covering the roots of the roses already laid in. See that the soil covers the roots both back and front, so that they do not lie hollow, tread slightly, and repeat the process as often as there are plants to lay in. Here the roses will remain without injury until required for planting even if planting is deferred for some weeks. Should the bundle arrive during a hard frost take it into the potting-shed and leave it there for a few days just as it is. It would, however, not be advisable to leave the bundle unpacked much longer than a week, for the sooner the plants are in the ground the better. In the process of unpacking see that the roots do not become dry, and if they do, dip both roots and wood in a tub of water before laying them in the trench.

REVEREND JOSEPH PEMBERTON, FROM *ROSES, THEIR HISTORY, DEVELOPMENT AND CULTIVATION*, 1920

Concerning the Soil

I WOULD earnestly assure the novice in Rose growing that if he really means to make the Rose his hobby, and to enjoy the ride, he must feed him liberally and regularly with old oats and beans. The Rose cannot be grown in its glory without frequent and rich manure; and again, I recommend that the best farmyard dung be applied towards the end of November, when the ground is dry and dug in in March, and that the surface dressing be administered at the beginning of June. And if neighbours, who are not true lovers of the Rose, expostulate, and condemn the waste, quote for their edification those true words of Victor Hugo, in *Les Misérables*, "the beautiful is as useful as the useful, perhaps more so."

Nevertheless, I must warn the young Rosarian that he may be too lavish in his application of manures. The enthusiastic tyro has been known to plant his Rose trees in a composition, made up half and half, of raw reeking manure and soil. The results have been disastrous; and when an explanation of the debility outside has been sought within the soil; it has been sadly seen that the little tender rootlets have been sore let and hindered by their rank unsavoury surroundings, and have made but a feeble growth.

Nor must the amateur keep the sunshine and the rain from the soil by covering it continuously with solid manures. One liberal application from the farmyard, laid on late in November or early in December (when the first frost makes a hard road for the wheelbarrow), and dug in about the middle of March, is ample, with the addition of some fertilising liquid, when the buds expand for efflorescence, and some slight mulching in times of excessive drought.

S. REYNOLDS HOLE, FROM *A BOOK ABOUT ROSES*, 1869

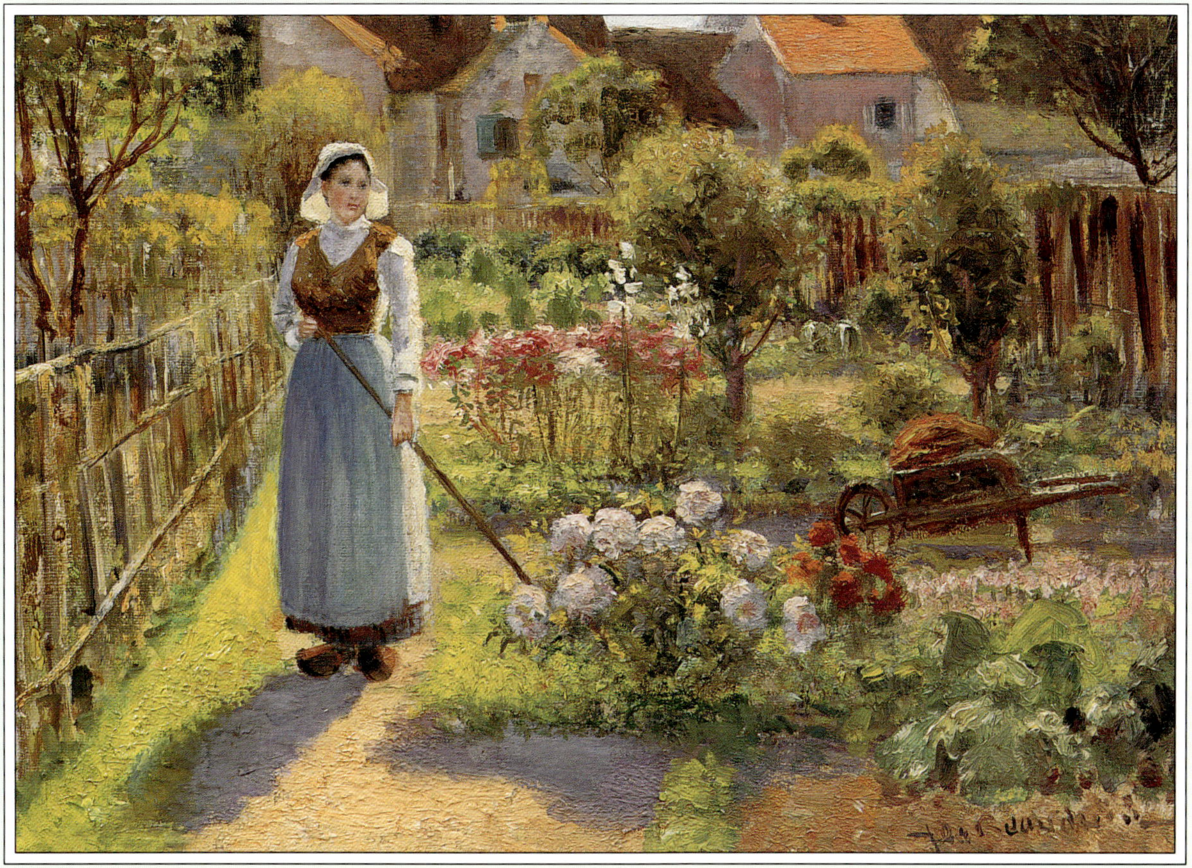

Propagating Roses

Every gardener, even the man with the small garden, loves his Roses, and many of them who take the trouble to think for themselves are wondering if it is wise to put in plants budded on stocks of whose rooting capabilities they are ignorant, and, moreover, there is their reaction to soil conditions and even their incompatability to the scions that are worked on them. In consequence there has arisen what looks like a new era in the propagation of Roses, for many amateurs are now raising their own plants by means of cuttings. When they do that they have the satisfaction of knowing that every plant has its own roots – no suckers of an alien to give any trouble – and they can treat their Roses accordingly.

The rooting of Rose cuttings is very simple, and as a matter of fact practically every Rose, with the possible exception of those of pure Pernet ancestry, can be struck and will emit strong roots. The best time for the insertion of cuttings is during the last half of October but the work can be equally well done in November. Cuttings should be made from the shoots that have flowered the previous June or July, and they should be about eight inches in length. Some growers like to take cuttings with a heel – that is a piece of the older wood – but it is not necessary. The best method of inserting the cuttings is to use a spade to cut a trench, and, unless your soil is light and open, some sand can be placed at the bottom. Insert the cuttings six inches deep, and make them very firm. You must watch them and make sure that they remain firm. If they become loosened they will assuredly not root. If you get a spell of frosty weather and a thaw sets in, you are almost certain to find that the cuttings have been drawn upwards. If that happens do not try to *push them down* again, or you will damage the base. Wait until the ground is thoroughly thawed and tread the ground to firm them again. I have to do that occasionally through the winter months.

When spring arrives a dry spell often sets in, and if that occurs you must make sure that the cuttings do not suffer from want of moisture for they are then at a critical period and are just throwing out young roots. Some of the cuttings may flower in late autumn. At the end of October, a year after insertion, the plants are ready for transference to the quarters where you wish them to flower.

George M. Taylor, from *The Little Garden*, 1948

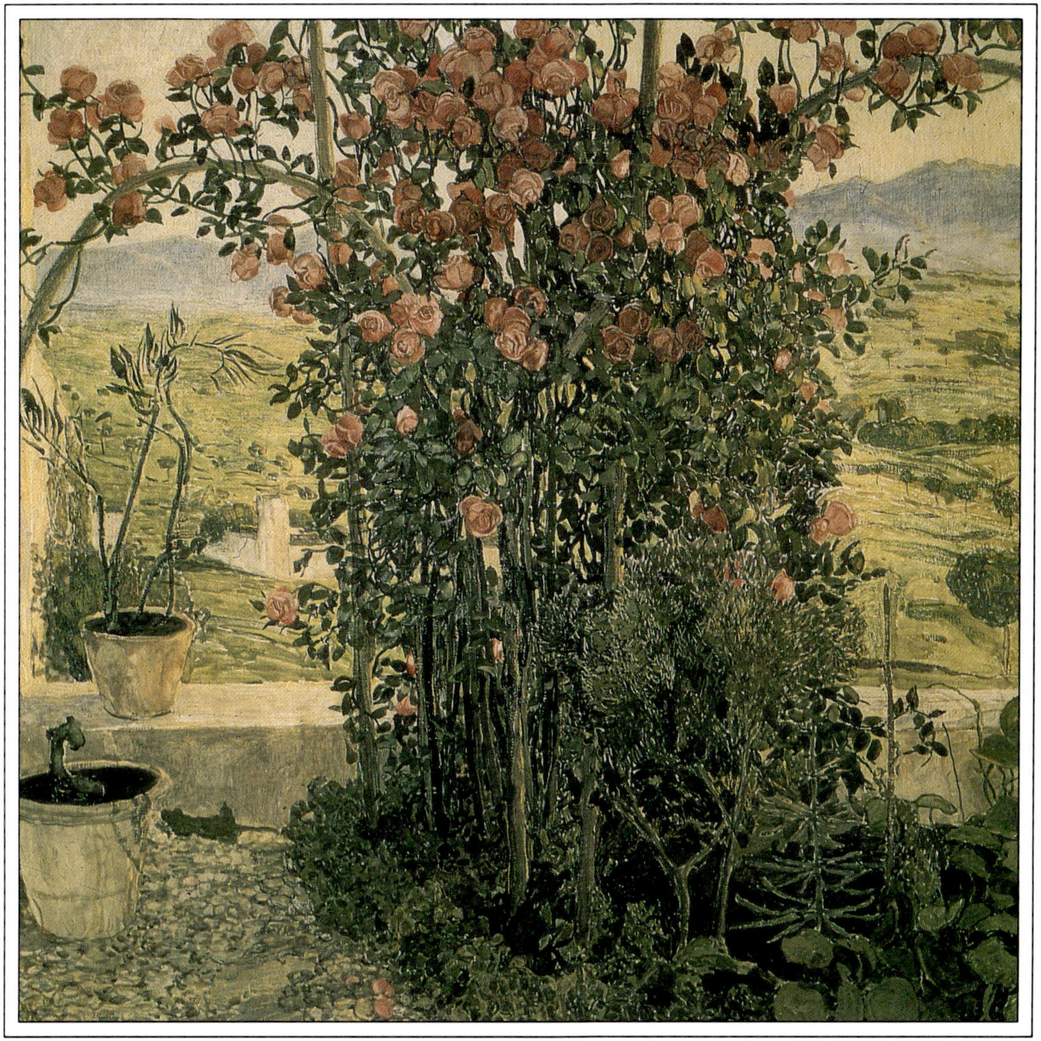

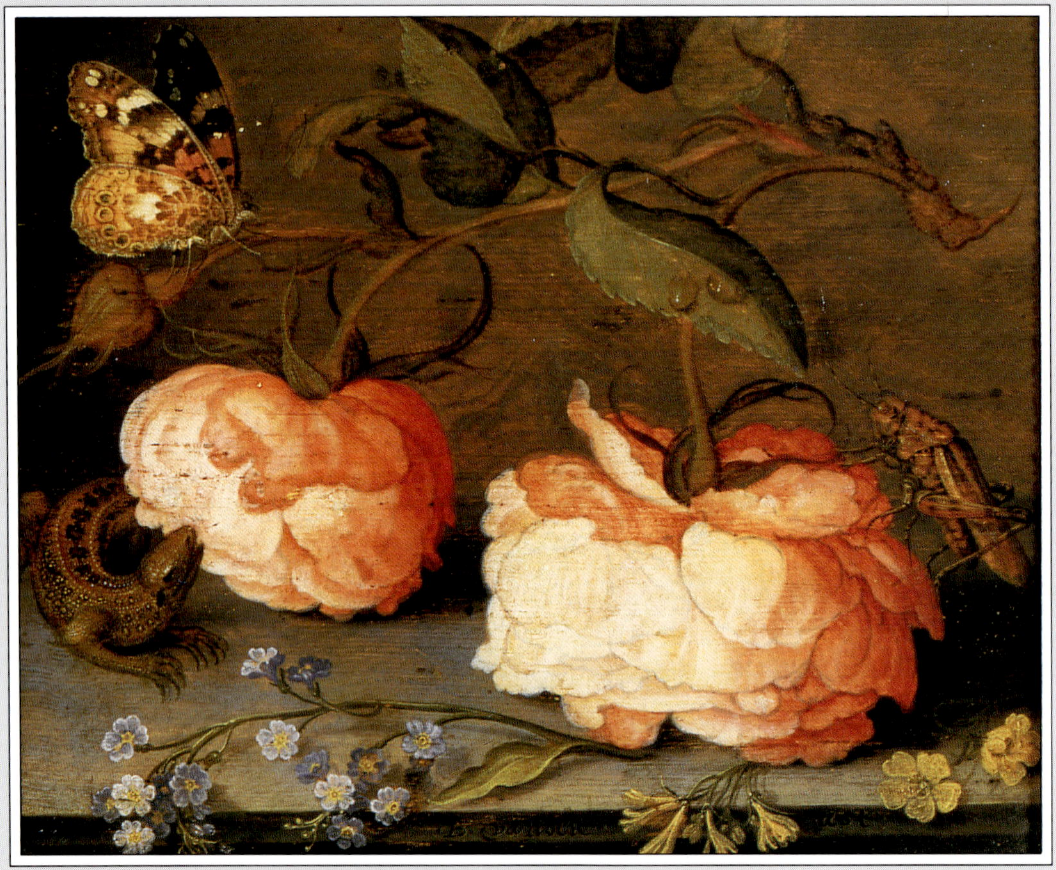

ENEMIES OF THE ROSE

CONSTANT care is requisite in spring and early summer to keep the shoots clear of caterpillars and grubs. These should be closely searched for while they are yet minute. They may be found sometimes eating into the bud before it has begun to expand; sometimes they attack the tender leaves, in which they provide themselves with dwellings by fastening the leaflets together, feeding all the time of their residence on the walls. When these are consumed, or are grown too coarse to supply them with food sufficiently delicate for their fastidious palates, they make their way to the young flower-buds, which they rapidly destroy. One species of grub nothing will satisfy but the tender pith of the youngest shoot. Into this it eats its way, and, without touching any vital part, excavates for itself a tubular dwelling-place, and is only detected when the mischief is done by the sudden withering of the shoot. These mischievous little creatures proceed from the eggs of certain small moths and saw-flies, some of which are deposited on the old wood during the previous year, and others from time to time after the buds have begun to swell. To prevent them from doing much harm, they should be caught and killed when they are not more than the eighth of an inch in length, and no thicker than a hair. They are in colour green or brown.

The little green flies (*aphides*) which infest the young shoots of roses may be destroyed by dipping the twigs into a basin of tobacco-water.

EDITED BY THE REV. C.A. JOHNS, FROM *GARDENING FOR CHILDREN*, 1848

Old Fashioned Roses

THE Old Rose amounts to an enormous literature in itself, and its enthusiasts are in wait round every corner, ready equipped for argument and contradiction. It would be quite impossible for an amateur with but a few years of experience to dispute the studies of a lifetime. For the Old Rose, this is certain, has, already, no lack of admirers. It is to them, in fact, that we appeal, hoping that they may listen in patience to our account of some other flowers that they may have neglected. For the Rose has that preponderance, that popularity and practicability, that is possessed, in the world of music, by the pianoforte. If all other musical instruments were banished the piano would still remain, in the words of Liszt, the 'maid-of-all-work of music'. It would still be possible, through the piano, as it would be through no other musical instrument, to obtain some idea of the pleasures of music: to the same degree, the Rose is the universal flower of all gardens. And, just as an ever-increasing public is learning to appreciate the harpsichord and the clavichord, is discovering Bach and Couperin and Domenico Scarlatti, Handel and the Elizabethan composers, as it were, in their original beauty, so the Old Fashioned Rose has, long ago, given a revelation to many persons of the loveliness of its old ideals.

SACHEVERELL SITWELL (1897–1988) FROM *OLD FASHIONED FLOWERS*

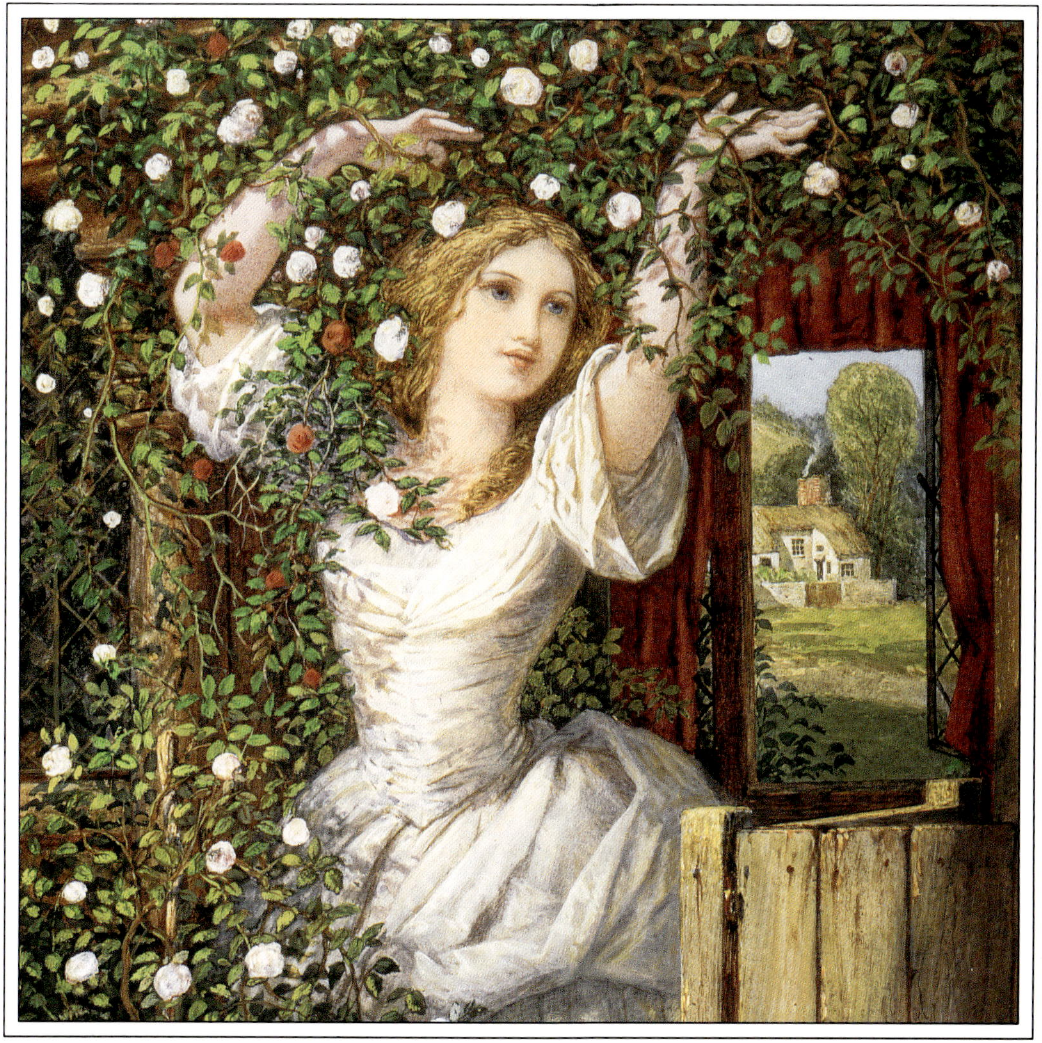

To the Virgins, to Make Much of Time

Gather ye rosebuds while ye may,
  Old Time is still a-flying:
And this same flower that smiles to-day
  To-morrow will be dying.

The glorious lamp of heaven, the sun,
  The higher he's a-getting,
The sooner will his race be run,
  And nearer he's to setting.

That age is best which is the first,
  When youth and blood are warmer;
But being spent, the worse, and worst
  Times still succeed the former.

Then be not coy, but use your time,
  And while ye may, go marry:
For having lost but once your prime,
  You may for ever tarry.

Robert Herrick (1591–1674)

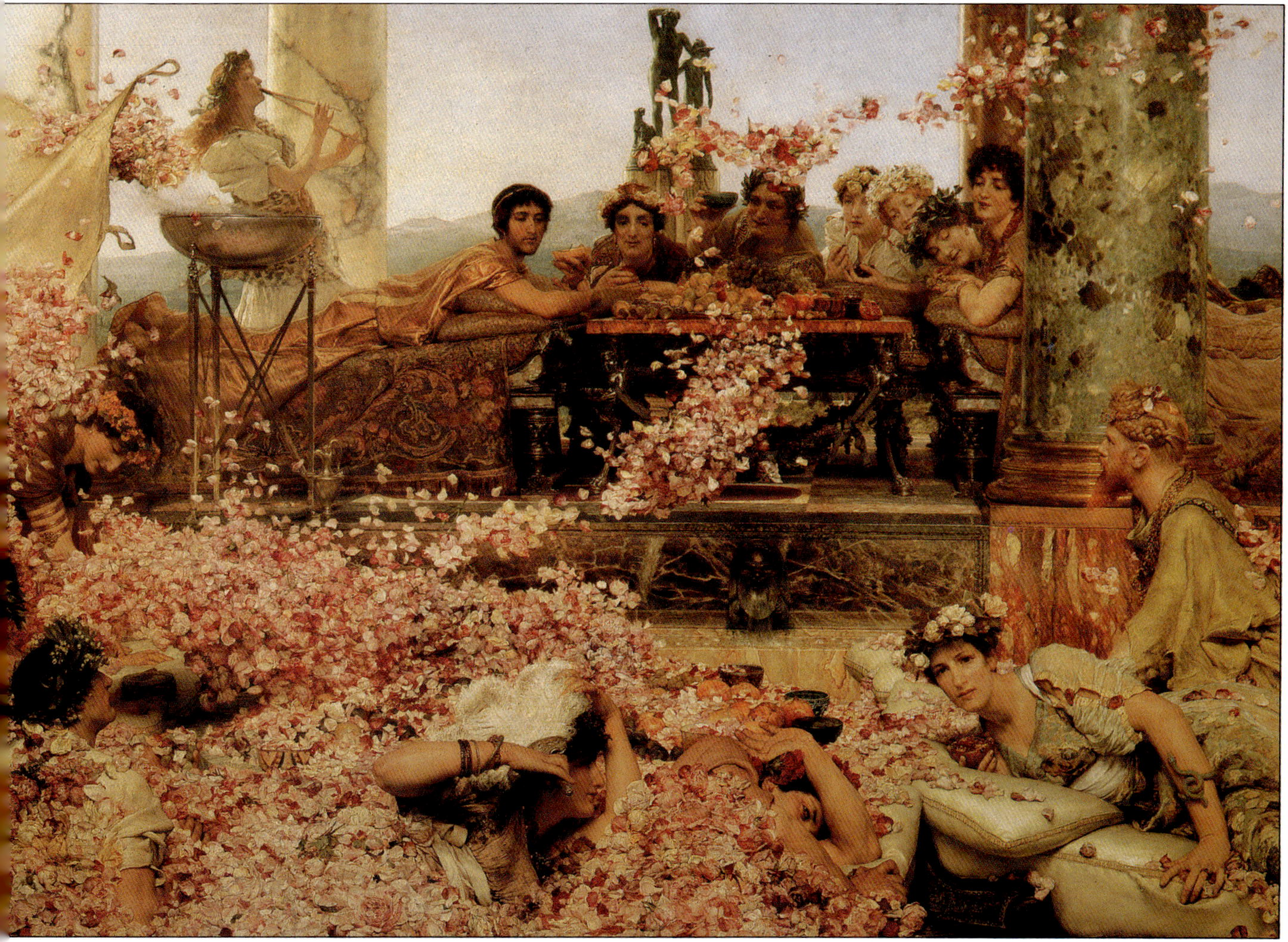

A Little Budding Rose

It was a little budding rose,
   Round like a fairy globe,
And shyly did its leaves unclose
   Hid in their mossy robe,
But sweet was the slight and spicy smell
It breathed from its heart invisible.

The rose is blasted, withered, blighted,
   Its root has felt a worm,
And like a heart beloved and slighted,
   Failed, faded, shrunk its form.
Bud of beauty, bonnie flower,
I stole thee from thy natal bower.

I was the worm that withered thee,
Thy tears of dew all fell for me;
Leaf and stalk and rose are gone,
Exile earth they died upon.
Yes, that last breath of balmy scent
With alien breezes sadly blent!

              EMILY BRONTË (1818–1848)

The Rose

A ROSE, as fair as ever saw the North,
   Grew in a little garden all alone;
A sweeter flower did Nature ne'er put forth,
Nor fairer garden yet was never known:
The maidens danced about it morn and noon,
And learnèd bards of it their duties made;
The nimble fairies by the pale-faced moon
Water'd the root and kiss'd her pretty shade.
But well-a-day! – the gardener careless grew;
The maids and fairies both were kept away,
And in a drought the caterpillars threw
Themselves upon the bud and every spray.
   God shield the stock! If heaven send no supplies,
   The fairest blossom of the garden dies.

WILLIAM BROWNE (1590–1645)

The Damask Rose

Near the Provence Rose, in sentiment as well as in a sort of natural garden classification, comes the Damask, charming also with its delicious though fainter scent and its wide-open crimson flowers. The Damask Rose, with some of the older Gallicas, may be considered the ancestors of many of our modern Roses, and though there is no record of the earlier pedigrees, those who are old enough to remember some of the first Hybrid Perpetuals will retain the recollection of some Roses such as Lee's Perpetual in which such parentage, probably passing through a Portland Rose, of which group there are a few named kinds, is fairly traceable. The parti-coloured form is a charming bush Rose that should be much more used; it is known by the names Rosa Mundi, Cottage Maid, and York and Lancaster. The latter name is also claimed for another striped Rose of much less value, but the name is so pretty and the Rose so charming that most of us think they ought to belong to each other, and that there is at least no harm in their association for general use.

GERTRUDE JEKYLL & EDWARD MAWLEY, FROM *ROSES FOR ENGLISH GARDENS*, 1902

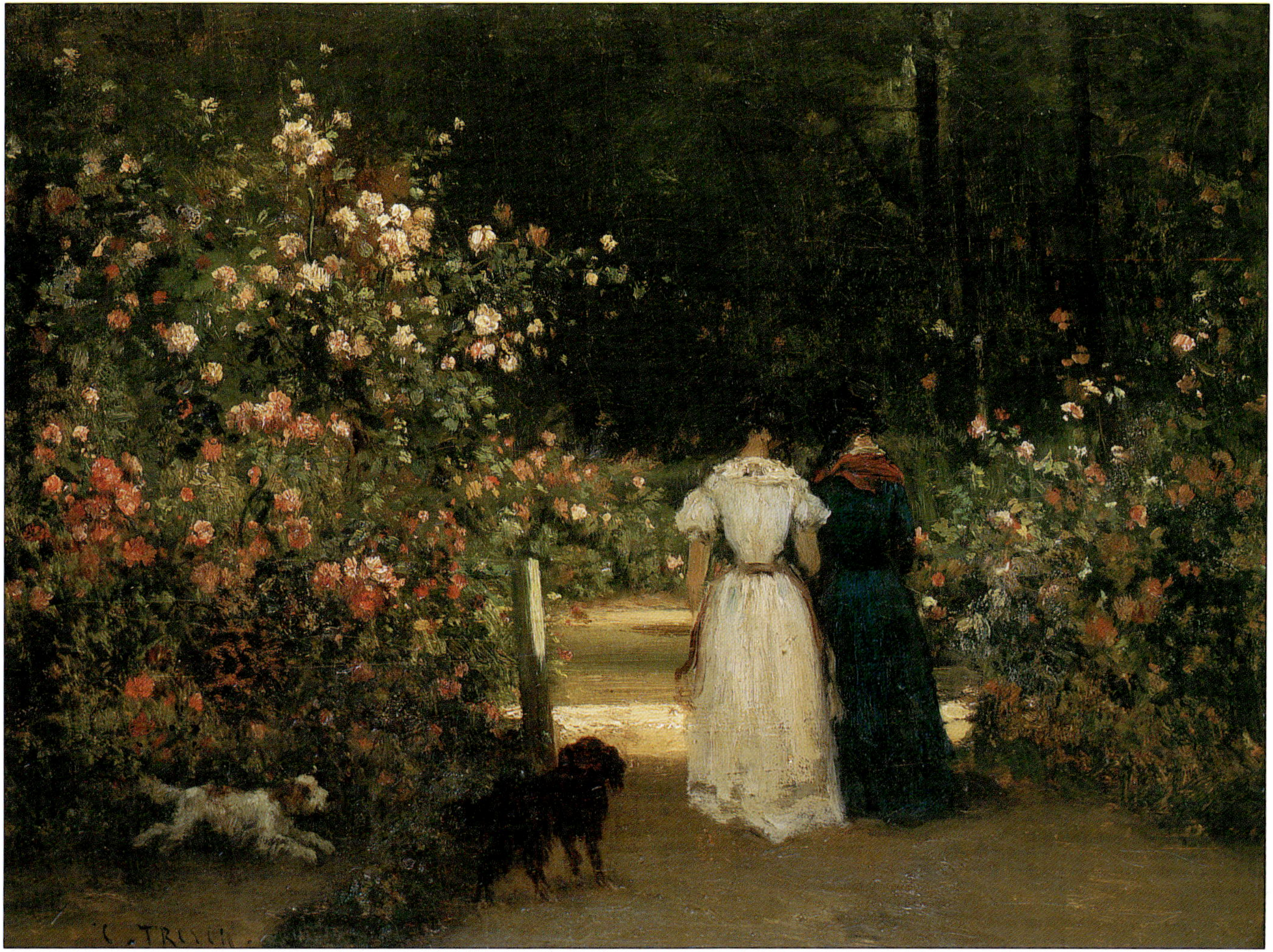

MAUD

Come into the garden, Maud,
    For the black bat, Night, has flown,
Come into the garden, Maud,
    I am here at the gate alone;
And the woodbine spices are wafted abroad,
    And the musk of the roses blown.

For a breeze of morning moves,
    And the planet of Love is on high,
Beginning to faint in the light that she loves
    On a bed of daffodil sky,
To faint in the light of the sun she loves,
    To faint in his light, and to die.

All night have the roses heard
    The flute, violin, bassoon;
All night has the casement jessamine stirr'd
    To the dancers dancing in tune;
Till a silence fell with the waking bird,
    And a hush with the setting moon.

I said to the rose, 'The brief night goes
    In babble and revel and wine.
O young lord-lover, what sighs are those
    For one that will never be thine?
But mine, but mine,' so I sware to the rose,
    'For ever and ever, mine.'

And the soul of the rose went into my blood,
    As the music clash'd in the hall;
And long by the garden lake I stood,
    For I heard your rivulet fall
From the lake to the meadow and on to the wood,
    Our wood, that is dearer than all;

The slender acacia would not shake
    One long milk-bloom on the tree;
The white lake-blossom fell into the lake,
    As the pimpernel dozed on the lea;
But the rose was awake all night for your sake,
    Knowing your promise to me;
The lilies and roses were all awake,
    They sigh'd for the dawn and thee.

Alfred Lord Tennyson (1809–1892)

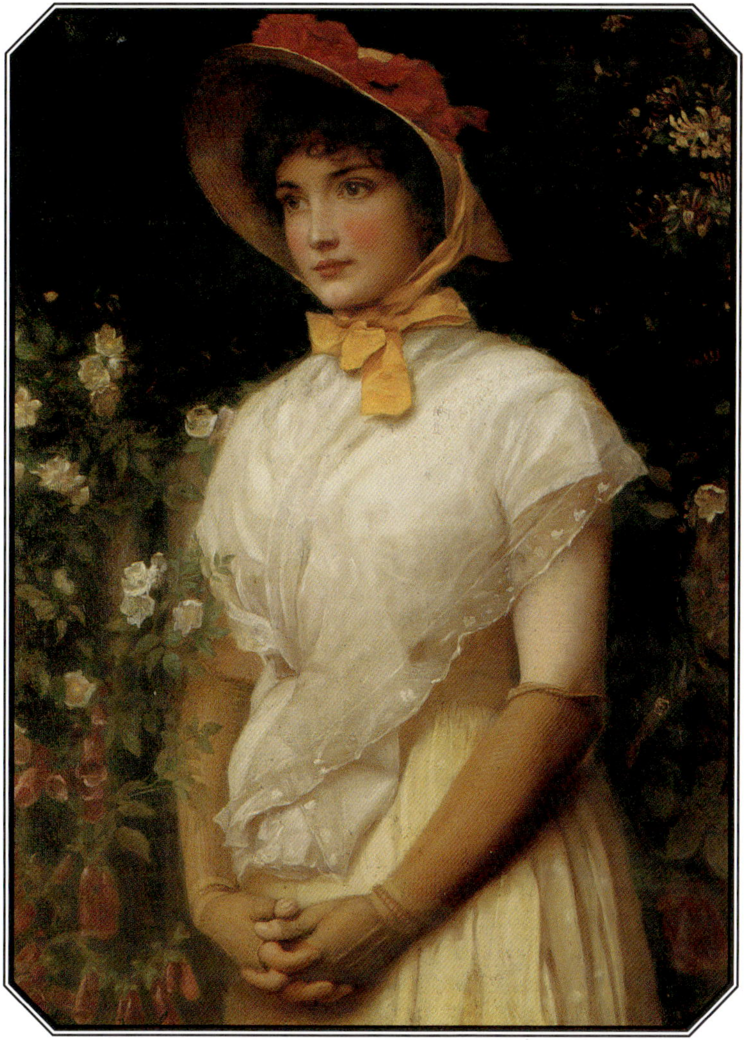

THE OLD ROSE

I AM writing in a rose garden; filled with the beauty of the roses, which for centuries have reigned in the gardens of princes and peasants alike and whose very names are full of romance. For centuries, these roses have held the secret of all that is sweetest and best in the home life of our race. Small wonder that the rose is our national flower, for it is the symbol of the home.

What modern roses can compare for beauty or for fragrance with these queens of ancient lineage? Look at a bowl of these roses in a room filled with treasures of art, and see how perfectly both in form and colour they are in keeping with pictures by the great masters, with priceless furniture and tapestries. Put the 'elegant' long stalked pointed modern hybrid teas in the same room and see how out of place they look. Or again, look at the old roses set in a crock on a cottage window sill. The queens are serenely and happily at home, whereas the modern upstarts would look even more ill at ease than before. The old roses blend perfectly not only with each other but with other flowers, even the humblest, but the modern roses do not blend even with each other.

ELEANOUR SINCLAIR ROHDE, FROM *THE SCENTED GARDEN*, 1931

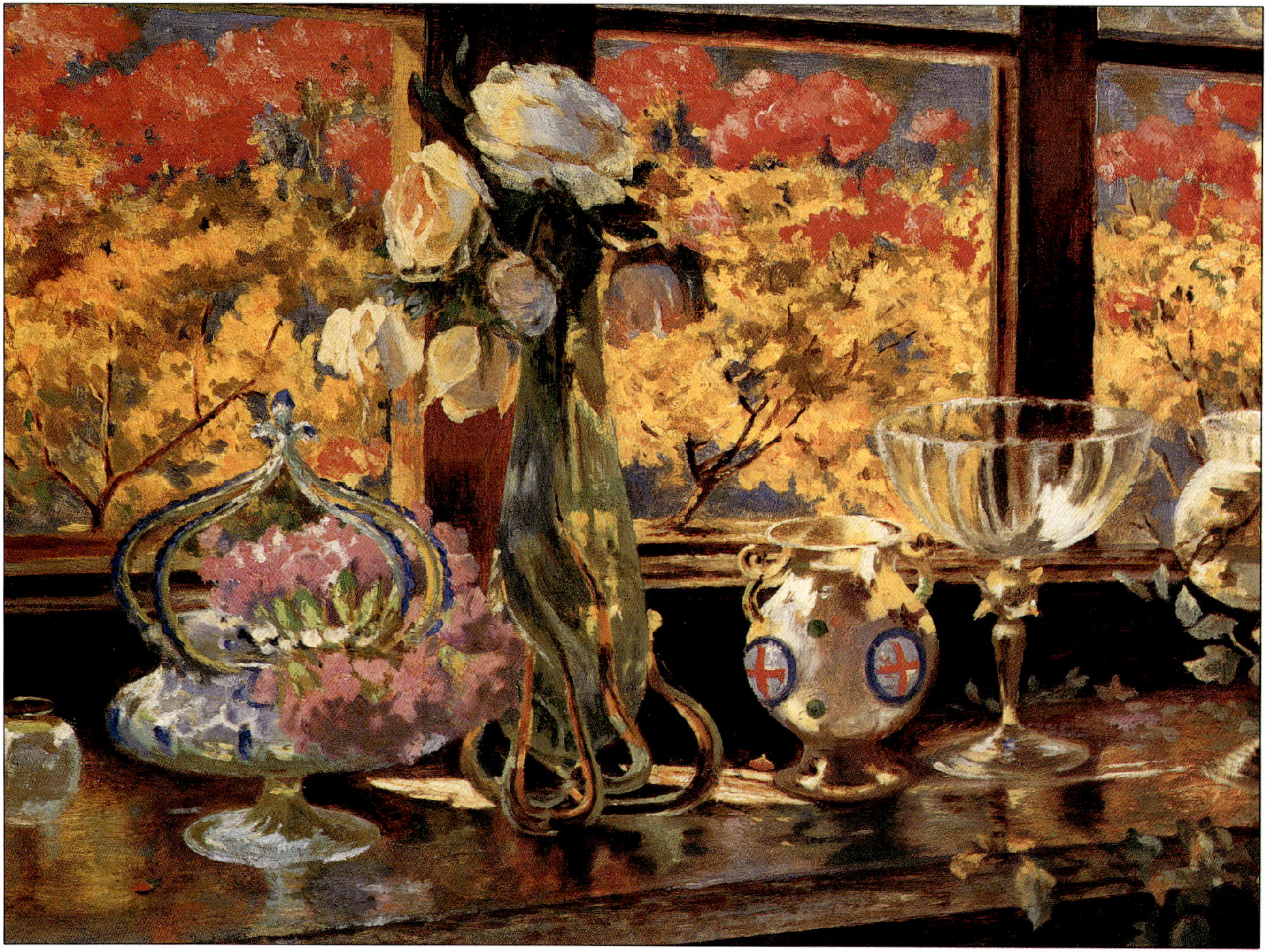

ROSES

Nature responds so beautifully.
  Roses are only once-wild roses, that were given an extra chance,
So they bloomed out and filled themselves with coloured fulness
Out of sheer desire to be splendid, and more splendid.

D.H. LAWRENCE (1885–1930)

THE ROSE FAMILY

THE rose is a rose,
 And was always a rose.
But the theory now goes
That the apple's a rose,
And the pear is, and so's
The plum, I suppose.
The dear only knows
What will next prove a rose.
You, of course, are a rose –
But were always a rose.

ROBERT FROST (1874–1963)

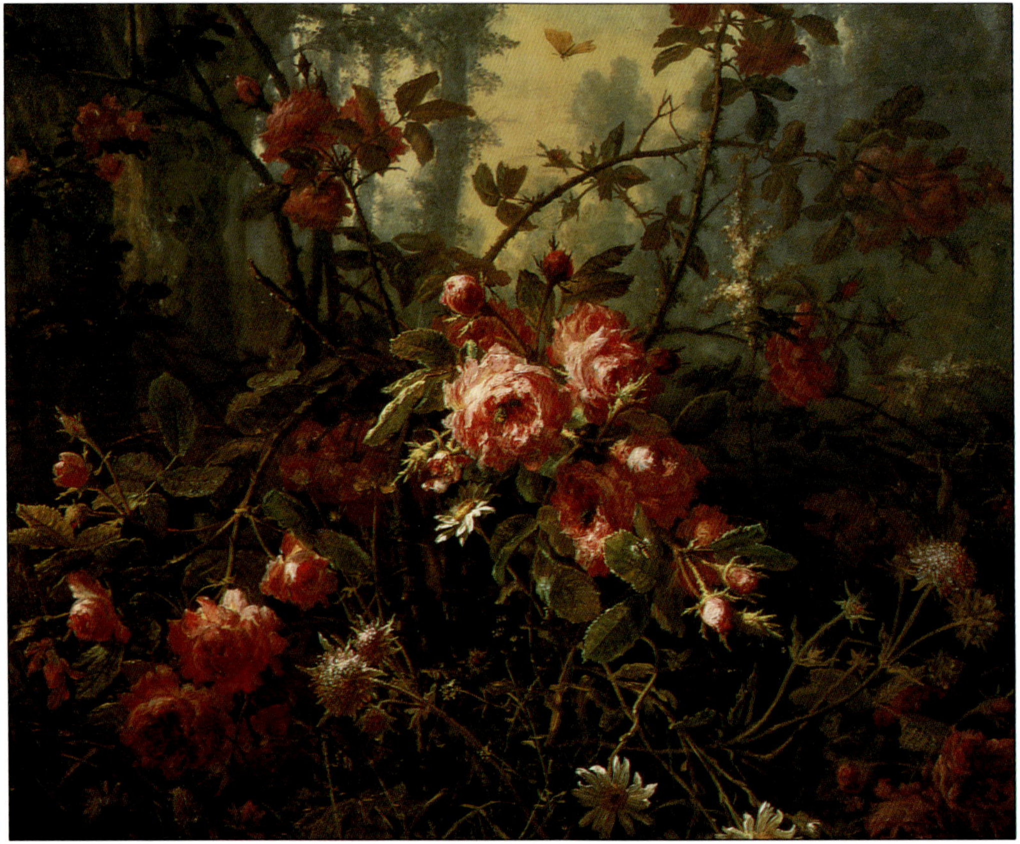

THE MOSS ROSE

The Victorian age would have seemed incomplete without the Moss Rose, so firmly did it entwine the hearts of those amiable days. Valentines and scrapbooks shared its portraits and its 'message' in the language of flowers. Before its day it would seem that no grace or charm could be added to the Rose, Beauty's last word had been said. But when it was found that the Rose could look cosy as well as beautiful by adding a little moss, no wonder that hearts were stormed. Cosiness lay at the very centre of Victorian taste.

The legend of the birth of the Moss Rose is found in a popular Calvados legend.

'One day the Angel, who each day brings the dew on her wings, feeling weary, asked the Rose for shelter for the night. On awakening, she asked how this hospitality might be repaid. The Rose answered, "Make me even more beautiful". "What grace", said the Angel, "can I give to the most beautiful of all flowers?" Meditating this request, she cast her eyes down to the mossy bed from which the Rose sprang and, gathering some, placed it on the young buds. Thus was born the Moss Rose.'

When from fancy we turn to fact, we find that the history of the Moss Rose is still somewhat of a mystery. We are quite sure that it is a Cabbage Rose which has added moss to its buds and shoots, as many times in history the Moss Rose has thrown out a sporting branch without moss, having all the marks of the Cabbage Rose.

EDWARD A. BUNYARD, 1936

An Old-World Corner

In planting climbing Roses there is always a danger of falling into the trap that so many amateurs succeed in doing. Because Dorothy Perkins is a very beautiful climber – and, indeed, so are all the Wichuriana class to which it belongs – it is used a little too freely. It should be remembered that this particular class flowers very late, and that its actual period of full beauty is comparatively short. It is well, therefore, to use Roses of other classes that flower later and earlier in fair proportions. These can be found among the free-growing Teas, hybrid Teas, Noisettes, Ramblers, Polyanthas, etc., and there are so many of them that to mention a few would be to do an injustice to the remainder. In every garden there should be reserved somewhere a space, perhaps only an odd corner, for a few of those freer-growing classes that are very beautiful, but, on account of their rampant growth, are too overpowering in any set scheme. Such are the Japanese Rosa Rugosa, the Austrian Briers, and the hybrids thereof; the old world Moss, Provence, Damask roses, some of which could have been found in the gardens of England any time during the last three hundred years or more. This old-world corner will always be interesting, with its Cabbage Rose, a sixteenth-century memory, White Provence, which dates from 1777, and York and Lancaster, which, with its white and red flowers, will carry back the memory to the turmoil of the fifteenth century.

GEORGE DILLISTONE, FROM *THE PLANNING AND PLANTING OF LITTLE GARDENS*, 1920

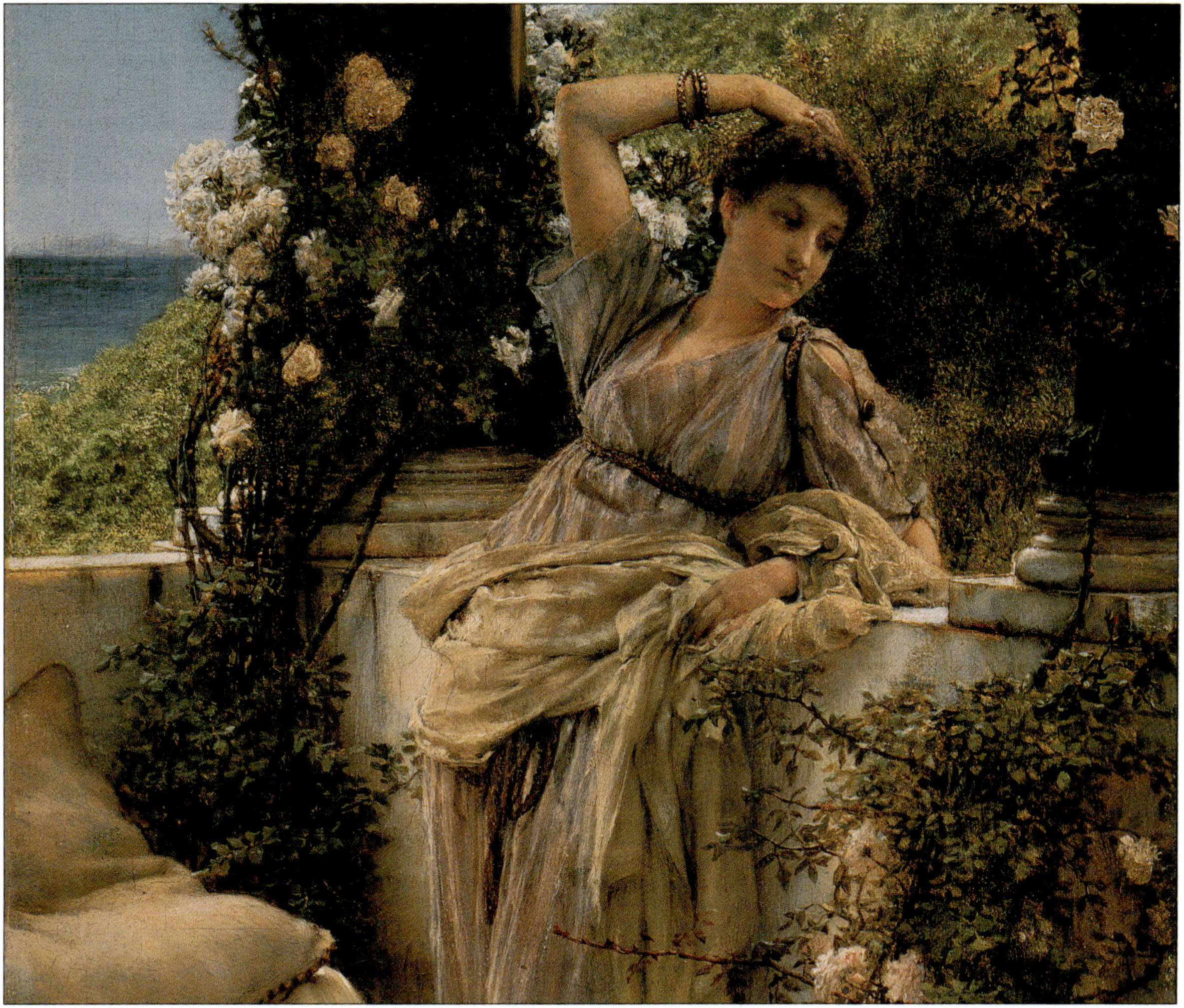

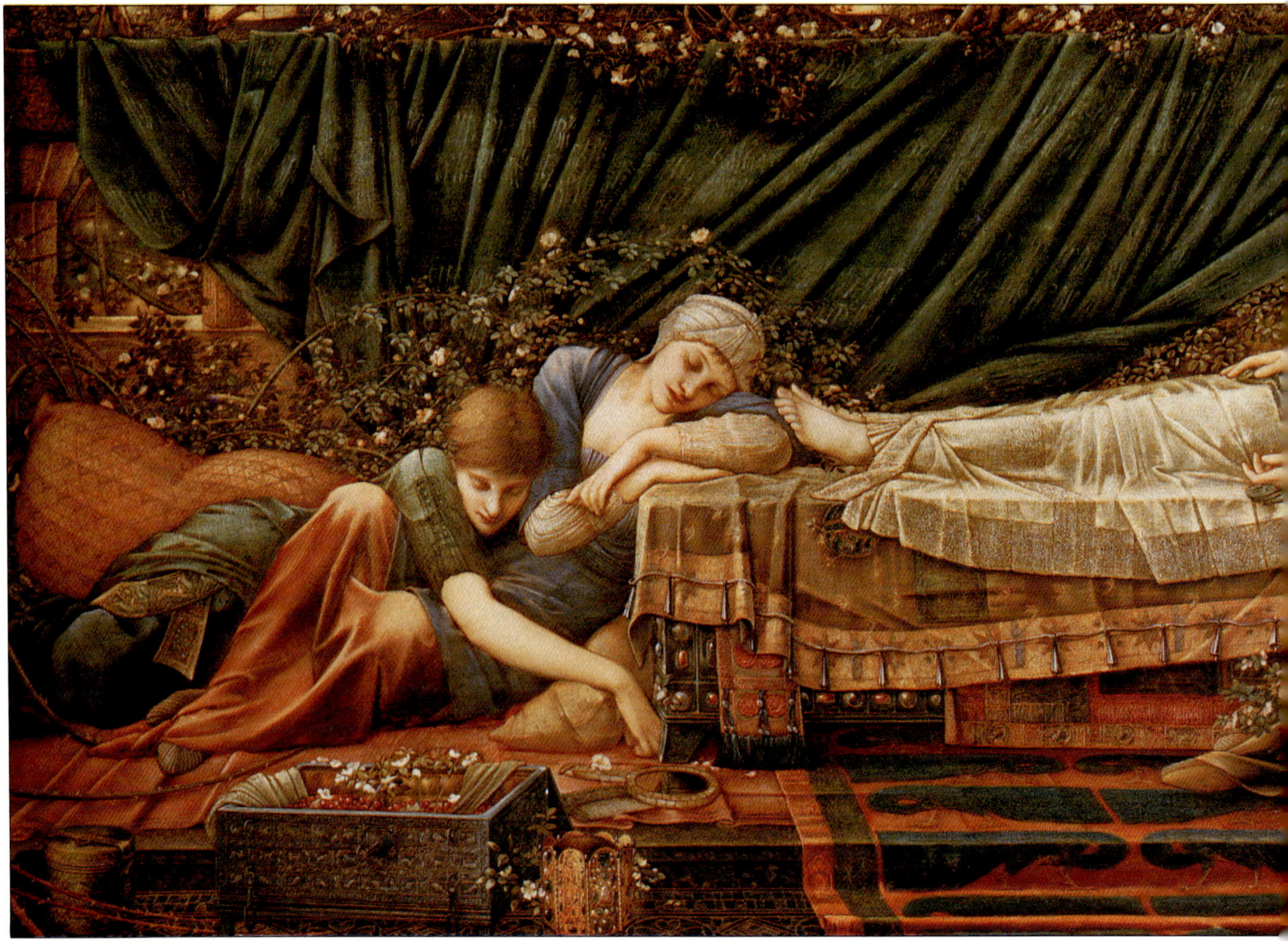

SONNET

Look, Delia, how w' esteem the half-blown rose,
    The image of thy blush and Summer's honour,
Whilst yet her tender bud doth undisclose
    That full of beauty time bestows upon her;
No sooner spreads her beauty in the air,
    But straight her wide-blown pomp comes to decline;
She then is scorned who late adorned the fair:
    So fade the roses in those cheeks of thine,
No April can revive the withered flowers,
    Whose springing grace adorns thy glory now;
Swift speedy time, feather'd with flying hours,
    Dissolves the beauty of the fairest brow.
Then do not thou such treasure waste in vain,
But love now, whilst thou mayest be loved again.

SAMUEL DANIEL (C. 1562)

ROSE AND CABBAGE

AND still I look for the men who will dare to be
    roses of England
wild roses of England
men who are wild roses of England
with metal thorns, beware!
but still more brave and still more rare
the courage of rosiness in a cabbage world
fragrance of roses in a stale stink of lies
rose-leaves to bewilder the clever fools
and rose-briars to strangle the machine.

                          D.H. LAWRENCE (1885–1930)

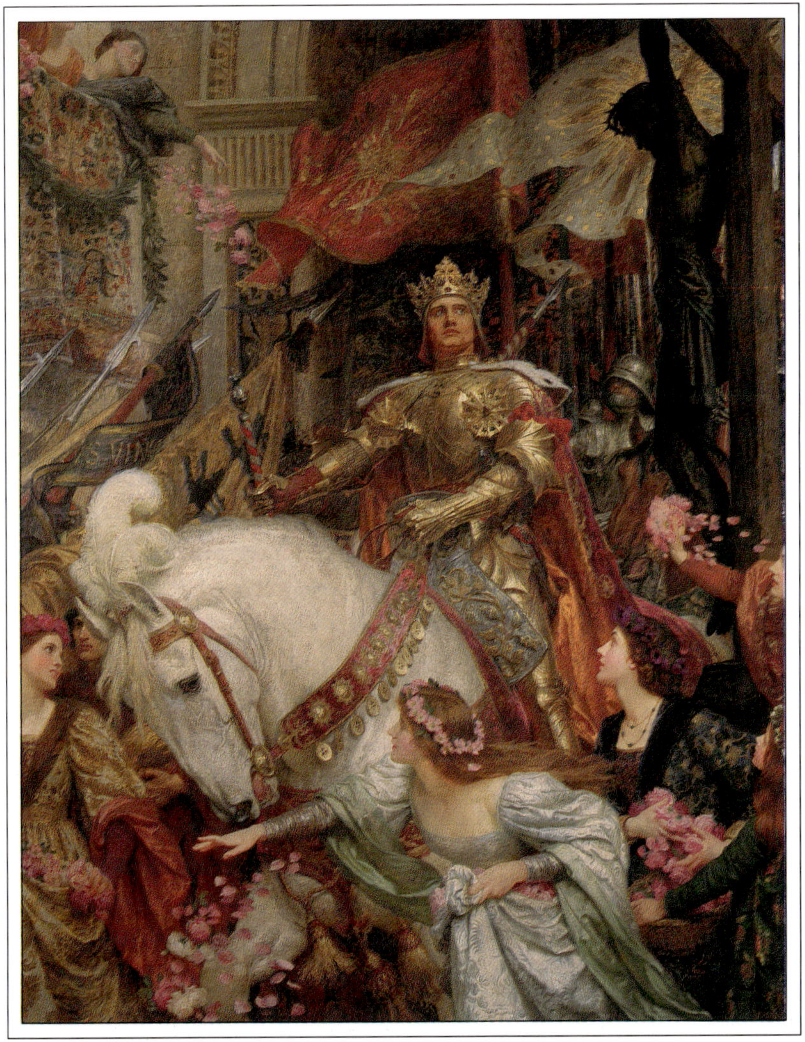

Sonnet 54

O, HOW much more doth beauty beauteous seem
   By that sweet ornament which truth doth give!
The rose looks fair, but fairer we it deem
For that sweet odour which doth in it live.
The canker-blooms have full as deep a dye
As the perfumed tincture of the roses,
Hang on such thorns, and play as wantonly
When summer's breath their masked buds discloses;
But for their virtue only is their show,
They lived unwoo'd, and unrespected fade;
Die to themselves. Sweet roses do not so:
Of their sweet deaths are sweetest odours made.
And so of you, beauteous and lovely youth,
When that shall fade, by verse distills your truth.

WILLIAM SHAKESPEARE (1564–1616)

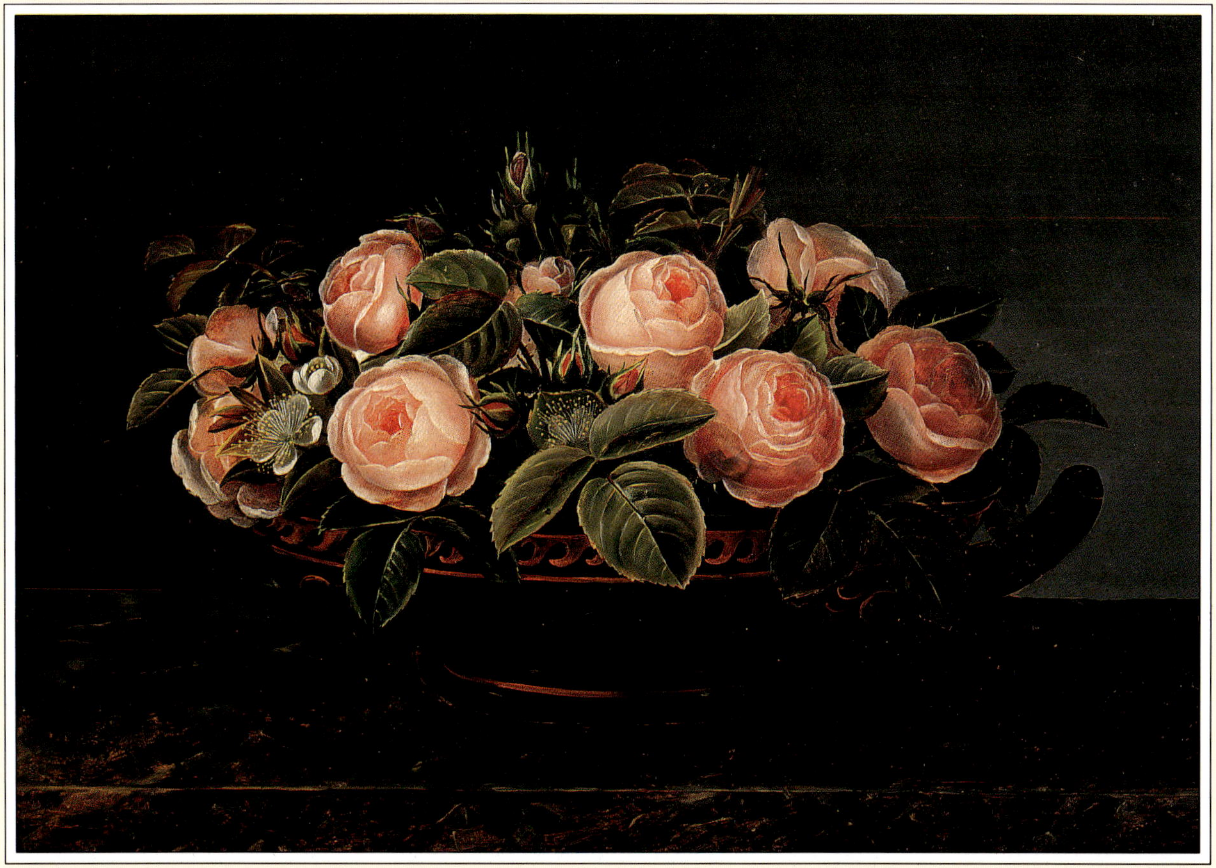

The Velvet Rose

There seems to have existed once a rose known as the Velvet Rose. Nobody knows with any certainty what particular rose was meant by this name, but it is supposed that it must have been a Gallica. Nobody knows the place of its origin: was it truly a wilding in Europe, or had it been imported into cultivation from the East? These are mysteries which have not as yet been resolved. All that we can say is that the name is very descriptive of its supposed descendants, amongst which we must include my favourite Tuscany.

The Velvet Rose. What a combination of words! One almost suffocates in their soft depths, as though one sank into a bed of rose-petals, all thorns ideally stripped away. We cannot actually lie on a bed of roses, unless we are very decadent and also very rich, but metaphorically we can imagine ourselves doing so when we hold a single rose close to our eyes and absorb it in an intimate way into our private heart. This sounds a fanciful way of writing, the sort of way which makes me shut up most gardening books with a bang, but in this case I am trying to get as close to my true meaning as possible. It really does teach one something, to look long and closely into a rose, especially such a rose as Tuscany, which opens flat (being only semi-double) thus revealing the quivering and dusty gold of its central perfection.

Vita Sackville-West (1892–1962) from *Some Flowers*

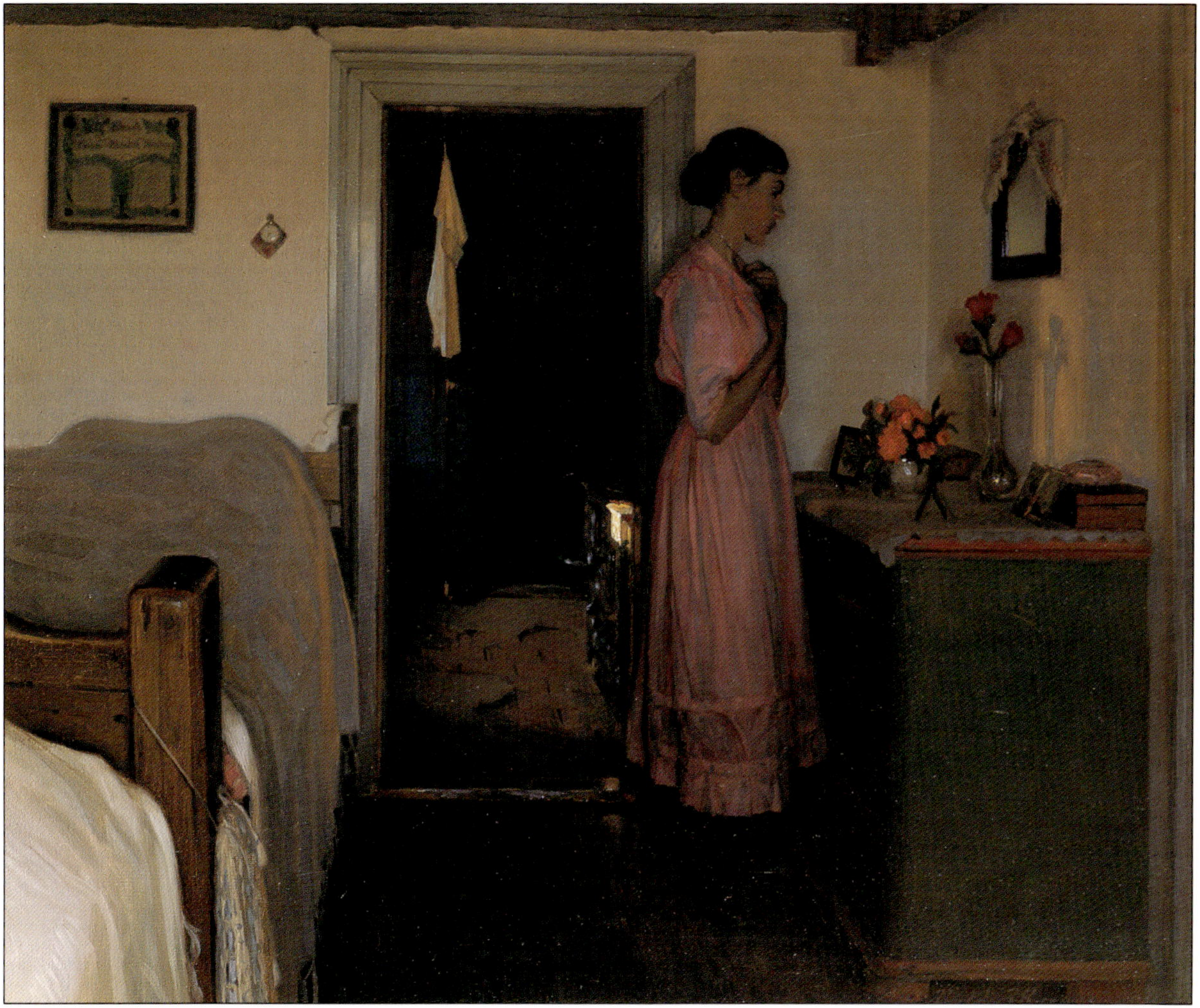

TO THE ROSE UPON THE ROOD OF TIME

RED Rose, proud Rose, sad Rose of all my days!
Come near me, while I sing the ancient ways:
Cuhoollin battling with the bitter tide;
The Druid, gray, wood-nurtured, quiet-eyed,
Who cast round Fergus dreams, and ruin untold;
And thine own sadness, whereof stars, grown old
In dancing silver sandalled on the sea,
Sing in their high and lonely melody.
Come near, that no more blinded by man's fate,
I find under the boughs of love and hate,
In all poor foolish things that live a day,
Eternal Beauty wandering on her way.

Come near, come near, come near – Ah, leave me still
A little space for the rose-breath to fill!
Lest I no more hear common things that crave;
The weak worm hiding down in its small cave,
The field mouse running by me in the grass,
And heavy mortal hopes that toil and pass;
But seek alone to hear the strange things said
By God to the bright hearts of those long dead,
And learn to chaunt a tongue men do not know.
Come near; I would, before my time to go,
Sing of old Eire and the ancient ways:
Red Rose, proud Rose, sad Rose of all my days.

W.B. YEATS (1865–1939)

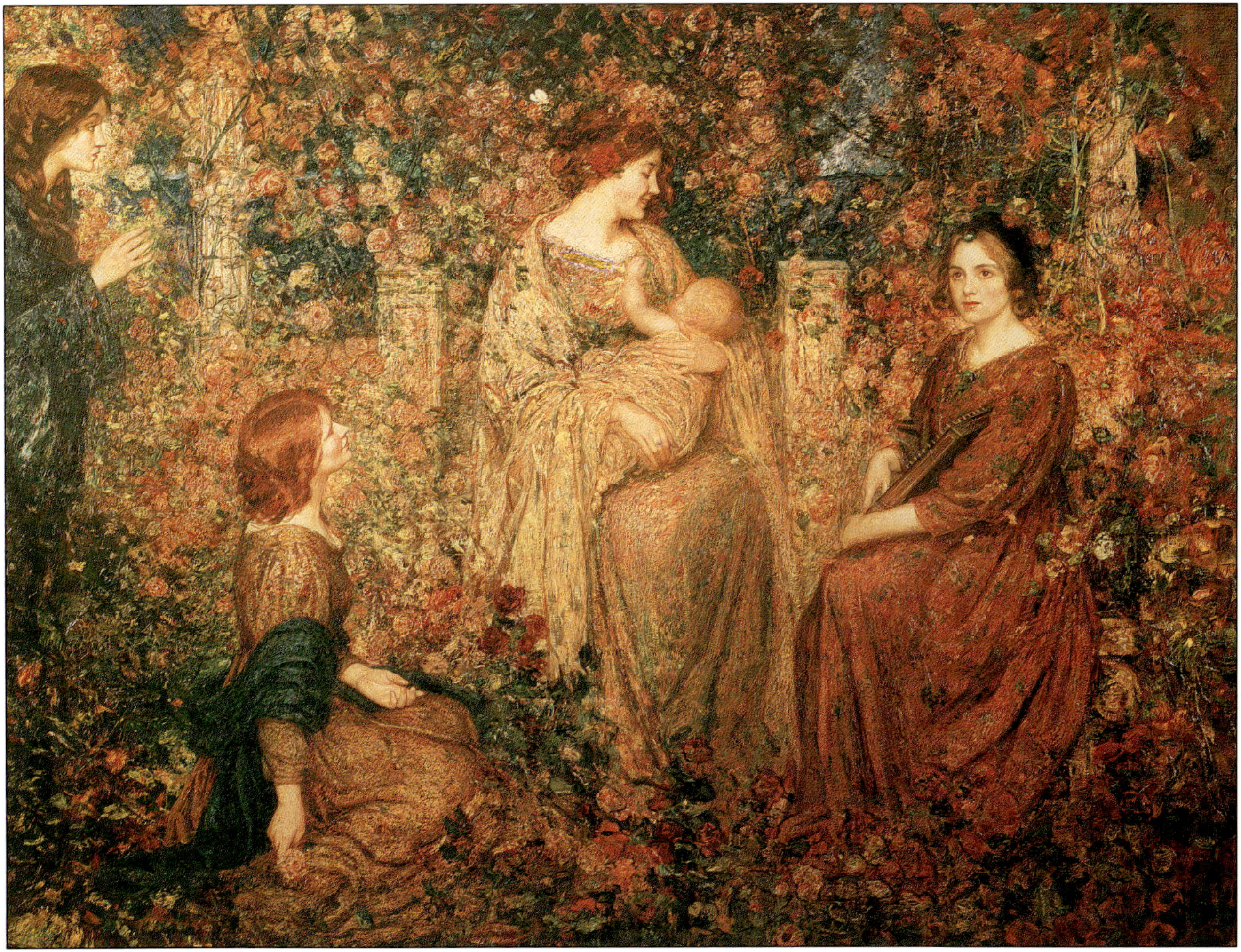

ROSES

You love the roses – so do I. I wish
    The sky would rain down roses, as they rain
    From off the shaken bush. Why will it not?
Then all the valley would be pink and white
And soft to tread on. They would fall as light
As feathers, smelling sweet: and it would be
Like sleeping and yet waking, all at once.

GEORGE ELIOT (1819–1880)

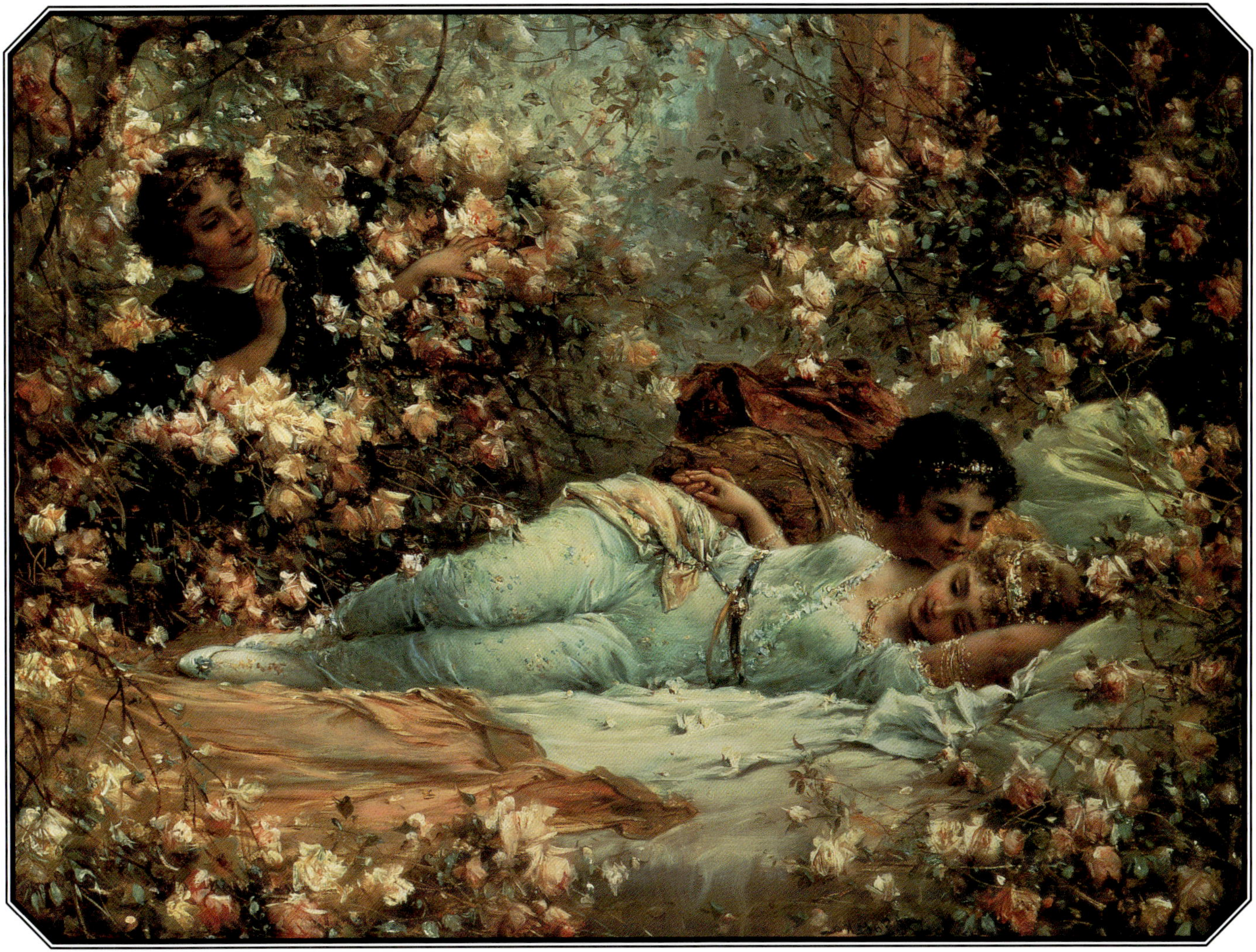

English Affections

So deep is the rose in English affections that to question its supremacy, or merely to find fault with some of the popular kinds, is to risk a charge of dullness almost amounting to depravity, of preaching a subversive doctrine. England itself, its cottages and country sentiment, all seem to be threatened by such behaviour. Gardeners of all classes delight to grow them; from the stockbroker with a whole acre of standard trees to the humblest suburban householder, none feels himself properly dressed without a flower of 'Shot Silk' or whatever the favourite of the moment may be.

WILLIAM BOWYER HONEY, FROM *GARDENING HERESIES AND DEVOTIONS*

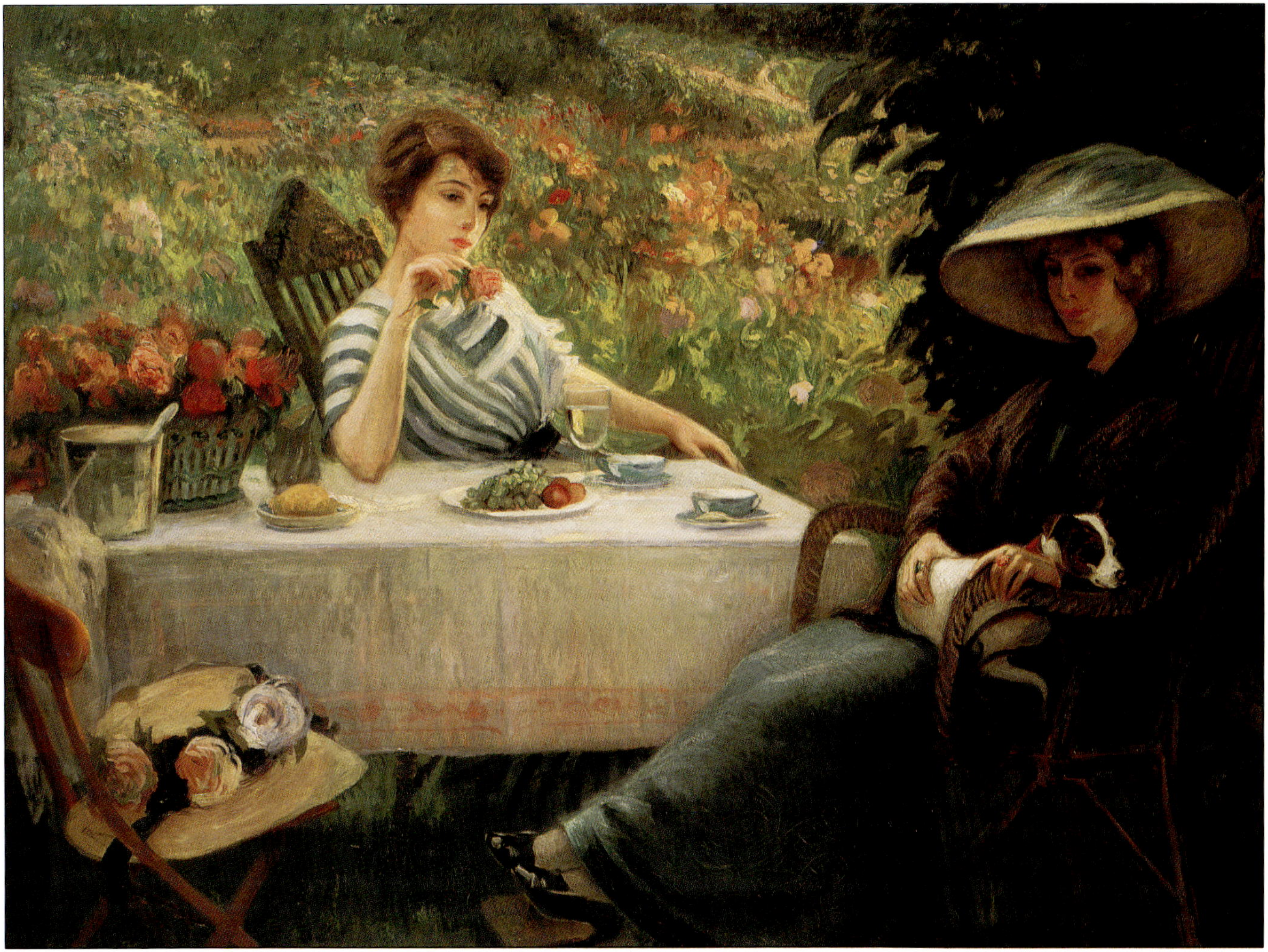

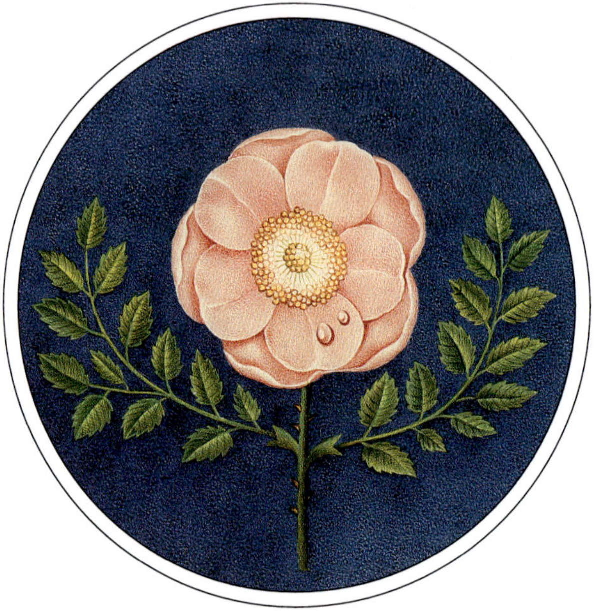

Penhaligon's Elisabethan Rose

The Sweet Scented Rose is scented with the delicate fragrance of Elisabethan Rose. It was created by Penhaligon's in 1985 and carries the true bouquet of an old-fashioned rose such as would have been found in an Elizabethan rose garden.

Our Elisabethan Rose has petals of palest pink, and a scent reminiscent of bygone days. To enjoy it fully, dear reader, please close your eyes, rub the endpapers of this book, and dream of sitting in an English rose garden on a still midsummer afternoon.

Sheila Pickles

For more information about Penhaligon's perfumes,
please telephone London (011 44 81) 880 2050 or write to:
PENHALIGON'S
41 Wellington Street
Covent Garden
London WC2

Acknowledgements

PICTURE ACKNOWLEDGEMENTS

Bridgeman Art Library, London:
p2 *Basket of Flowers*: Hans Looscher/Gavin Graham Gallery, London; p4 *Portrait of a Young Girl Holding a Bunch of Roses*: Alexei Alexeiwitsch/Private Collection; p9 *Young Girls with Roses*: Sir Lawrence Alma Tadema/Private Collection; p11 *The Sun in May*: Josef Mehoffer/Private Collection: p13 *Choosing the Red and White Roses in Temple Gardens*: Henry Payne/Birmingham City Museums and Art Gallery; p 14 *The Earl of Pembroke*: Peter Oliver/V&A, London; pl5 *Flora*: Titian, Tiziano (Vecellio)/Galleria Degli Uffizi, Florence; pl7 *The Buffet*: Jean Louis Forain/Federation Mutualiste Parisienne, Paris; p23 *Breakfast on the Terrace*: Joseph Milner Kite/Whitford & Hughes, London; p24 *In Full Bloom*: Henry Arthur Bonnefoy/Haynes Fine Art at the Bindery Galleries, Broadway, Worcs.; p27 *The Garden*: Ethel Walker/Bradford Art Galleries & Museums; p28 *Woman with a Rose*: Pierre Auguste Renoir/Christie's, London; p29 *The Time of Wild Roses, Paddington Mill Pond, Surrey*: Edward Wilkins Waite/Private Collection; p30 *The Rose Garden*: John Arthur Black: Christopher Wood Gallery, London; p33 *Roundscliffe-Everywhere are Roses*: George Samuel Elgood/Christopher Wood Gallery, London; p37 *The Sundial, Brook House, Sussex-October*: Beatrice Parsons/Chris Beetles Ltd., London; p43 *The White Tablecloth*: Henri Eugene Augustin Le Sidaner/Private Collection; p47 *In a Galloway Rose Garden*: Hugh Monro/Whitford & Hughes, London; p52 *Reading*: Joseph Marius Avy/Whitford & Hughes, London; p57 *Valley in Umbria*: Alexander Golovin/Pushkin Museum, Moscow; p58 *A Still Life with Roses on a Ledge*: Balthasar van der Ast/Philips, The International Fine Art Auctioneers; p61 *The Rose Bower*: Edward Henry Wehnert/Philips, The International Fine Art Auctioneers; p62 *The Roses of Heliogabalus*: Sir Lawrence Alma-Tadema/Private Collection; p65 *In the Garden*: Sir Hubert von Herkomer/Bonhams, London; p72 *Books*: Catherine M Wood/Christopher Wood Gallery, London; p73 *An English Rose*: Joseph Clark/Galerie George, London; p77 *Thou Rose of all the Roses*: Sir Lawrence Alma-Tadema/Private Collection; p78 *The Sleeping Beauty. The Briar Rose Series 4*: Sir Edward Burne-Jones/Faringdon Collection, Buscot, Oxon.; p83 *Still life of Pink Roses*: School of Johan Laurents Jensen/Bonham's, London; p85 *A Moment's Reflection*: Valdemar Kornerup/Waterhouse & Dodd, London; p87 *The Child*: Tom Mostyn/Charles Young Fine Paintings, London; p89 *The Rose Bower*: H. Zatka/Josef Mensing Gallery, Hamm-Rhynern; p91 *Tea Time*: Jacques Jourdan/Gavin Graham Gallery, London.

Fine Art Photographs, London:
p7 *Pruning Roses*: Robert James Gordon; p19 *The Perfume Makers*: Ernst Rudolph; p20 *Roses*: George Smith; p22 *A Still life of Roses in a Basket*: L. Roussel; p35 *The Rose Bush*: Christine Marie Loumand; p39 *Peeling Vegetables*: Fanny Fildes; p41 *Billing and Cooing*: Carl Vilhelm Balsgaard; p49 *Larramet De Belot*: August-Louis Lepere; p51 *In the Rose Garden*: Thomas James Lloyd; p55 *Tending the Garden*: Jean Beauduin; p64 *Cupid's Mesh*: Robert Walker Macbeth; p67 *A Walk in the Rose Garden*: Constant Troyan; p69 *In the Flower Garden*: James N Lee; p71 *Still Life*: attributed to Louis Comfort Tiffany; p74 *A Study of Pink Roses and Butterflies*; p 75 *The Spirit of Night* (detail): John Atkinson Grimshaw.

Tate Gallery, London:
p45 *Roman de la Rose*: Dante Gabriel Rossetti; p81 *The Two Crowns*: Sir Frank Dicksee.

Cover: *The Rose Bower*: Edward Henry Wehnert/Philips the International Fine Art Auctioneers/Bridgeman Art Library, London.
Background and Endpapers: *Sweet Briar*: John Henry Dearle/Published by Permission of Arthur Sanderson & Sons Ltd.

TEXT ACKNOWLEDGEMENTS

The following extracts were reproduced by kind permission of the following publishers, copyright holders and agents.

p21 Extract from *Onward and Upward in the Garden* by Katharine S. White. Copyright © 1979 by E.B. White, Executor of the Estate of Katharine S. White. Reprinted by permission of Farrar, Straus & Giroux, Inc.

p22 'A Bowl of Roses' by Lawrence Durrell from *Collected Poems 1931-1971*. Reprinted in the UK by permission of Faber and Faber Ltd., and in the USA by Viking Penguin, a division of Penguin Books USA Inc. Copyright © 1953 by Lawrence Durrell, from *Lawrence Durrell: Collected Poems 1931 – 1974*. Edited by James A. Brigham.

p48 Extract from *In Your Garden* by Vita Sackville-West © Nigel Nicolson.

p73 'The Rose Family' by Robert Frost from *The Poetry of Robert Frost*, edited by Edward Connery Latham. Copyright © 1956 by Robert Frost. Copyright 1928, © 1968 by Henry Holt and Company, Inc. Reprinted in the UK by permission of Jonathan Cape.

p84 Extract from *Some Flowers* by Vita Sackville-West © Nigel Nicolson.

Selection and introduction copyright © 1994 by Sheila Pickles

Designed by Bernard Higton
Picture research by Lynda Marshall

All rights reserved. No part of this publication may be reproduced or transmitted in any form or by any means, electronic, or mechanical, including photocopying, recording, or by any information storage and retrieval system, without permission in writing from the publisher.

Published by Harmony Books,
a division of Crown Publishers, Inc.,
201 East 50th Street, New York, New York 10022.
Member of the Crown Publishing Group.
Random House, Inc., New York, Toronto, London, Sydney, Auckland.
Published in Great Britain by Pavilion Books in 1994.

Harmony and colophon are trademarks of
Crown Publishers, Inc.

Manufactured in Singapore by Tien Wah

Library of Congress Cataloging-in-Publication Data:

Sweet scented rose : a treasury of verse and prose / edited by Sheila Pickles ; scented by Penhaligon's. — 1st ed.
   p. cm.
  1. Roses—Literary collections. 2. Scented books—Specimens.
I. Pickles, Sheila.
PN6071.R58S94 1994
820.8'036—dc20   93–25562
                                                                  CIP

ISBN 0-517-59681-4

First American Edition

10 9 8 7 6 5 4 3 2 1